Identifying Ignitable Liquids in Fire Debris

Identifying Ignitable Liquids in Fire Debris

A Guideline for Forensic Experts

Jeanet Hendrikse
Netherlands Forensic Institute, The Hague, The Netherlands

Michiel Grutters
Netherlands Forensic Institute, The Hague, The Netherlands

Frank Schäfer
Bundeskriminalamt, Wiesbaden, Germany

ELSEVIER

AMSTERDAM • BOSTON • HEIDELBERG • LONDON
NEW YORK • OXFORD • PARIS • SAN DIEGO
SAN FRANCISCO • SINGAPORE • SYDNEY • TOKYO

Academic Press is an imprint of Elsevier

Academic Press is an imprint of Elsevier
125, London Wall, EC2Y 5AS
525 B Street, Suite 1800, San Diego, CA 92101-4495, USA
225 Wyman Street, Waltham, MA 02451, USA
The Boulevard, Langford Lane, Kidlington, Oxford OX5 1GB, UK

Notices
Knowledge and best practice in this field are constantly changing. As new research and
experience broaden our understanding, changes in research methods or professional practices,
may become necessary.

Practitioners and researchers must always rely on their own experience and knowledge in
evaluating and using any information or methods described herein. In using such information or
methods they should be mindful of their own safety and the safety of others, including parties for
whom they have a professional responsibility.

To the fullest extent of the law, neither the Publisher nor the authors, contributors, or editors,
assume any liability for any injury and/or damage to persons or property as a matter of products
liability, negligence or otherwise, or from any use or operation of any methods, products,
instructions, or ideas contained in the material herein.

ISBN: 978-0-12-804316-5

Library of Congress Cataloging-in-Publication Data
A catalog record for this book is available from the Library of Congress

British Library Cataloguing-in-Publication Data
A catalogue record for this book is available from the British Library

For Information on all Academic Press publications
visit our website at http://store.elsevier.com/

ELSEVIER   Book Aid International

Working together
to grow libraries in
developing countries

www.elsevier.com • www.bookaid.org

CONTENTS

ACKNOWLEDGMENTS

The idea for this Guideline arose several years ago at an annual meeting of the Fire & Explosions Investigation Working Group (FEIWG) of the European Network of Forensic Science Institutes (ENFSI). What began as a single page document, has, by our enthusiasm, eventually evolved into this current book.

We thank all of our European fire debris colleagues, for the support they gave and the interest they showed during the writing of this book, and for their support in publishing it.

Special thanks must go to Dr Ursula Hendriks from the Landeskriminalamt in Berlin (Germany), Xavier Archer from the Laboratoire Central de la Prefecture de Police in Paris (France), and Leo Peschier from the Netherlands Forensic Institute in The Hague (the Netherlands) for their time and effort in reviewing the book and providing valuable suggestions, questions, and comments, and also to Dr Silke Cox from the Bundeskriminalamt in Wiesbaden (Germany) for her work in editing and rewriting the text where necessary.

Last but not least, we thank Elizabeth Brown from Elsevier Academic Press, who believed in our work and offered the possibility to publish it.

Jeanet Hendrikse
Michiel Grutters
Frank Schäfer

The identification of ignitable liquid residues in fire debris samples can be a difficult and challenging task. It requires a broad knowledge of ignitable liquid products, combustion products, and other possible interferences, as well as the limitations of the analytical methods employed.

Knowledge of the variation in composition of the many ignitable liquid products on the market is necessary to identify them in fire debris samples. Knowledge on substrates that may contain (residues of) an ignitable liquid as an ingredient is necessary to determine the evidential value of the fire debris analysis results obtained. Knowledge of the effect of surrounding conditions on the composition of an ignitable liquid is important to avoid false negative identifications. Knowledge on background interferences that may be released from burnt and/or pyrolyzed substrate materials is important to avoid false positive identifications. Last but not least, knowledge of the limitations imposed by recovery and analysis method(s) is important to avoid false positive identifications and/or erroneous classifications of the identified products.

The compositions of numerous ignitable liquid formulations and common background interferences are illustrated in literature. Some guidelines which describe (minimum) criteria for the identification of ignitable liquids in fire debris samples can also be found in the literature. However, most, if not all, of these publications lack background information on the origin of the characteristics of these ignitable liquid products, that can serve as guidance for identifying them in fire debris. The authors of this document therefore felt the need to establish a guideline that discusses, and in particular, illustrates the characteristics of different ignitable liquid products in more detail. This guideline builds on the minimum criteria of the ignitable liquid classes defined in the internationally accepted standard ASTM E1618 "Standard Test Method for Ignitable Liquid Residues in Extracts from Fire Debris Samples by Gas Chromatography-Mass Spectrometry", which is used as the base document by many fire debris experts around the world.

This guideline discusses and illustrates in more detail the characteristics of, and the variation in, chemical composition of different classes of the ignitable liquid products defined by ASTM E1618:14 as well as the effects that have an impact on their compositions. For some product classes supportive identification criteria are suggested that could be particularly helpful in situations of doubt. Furthermore, this guideline provides general background information on the origin and the production of different ignitable liquid products.

It reflects the current knowledge of the authors on the production and composition of ignitable liquid products and substrates. The examples presented are not exhaustive and the composition of particular products may change in time due to changes in existing or new refinery and/or production processes.

This guideline is intended for chemists who are involved in fire debris analysis. It can be used as a model for an in-house document to include a different national classification scheme covering a range of products manufactured to local specifications not encountered elsewhere.

Jeanet N. Hendrikse, MSc

Jeanet Hendrikse is a forensic scientist at the Netherlands Forensic Institute (NFI) in The Hague, the Netherlands, a position she has held since 2004. She is a forensic expert in the fields of fire debris analysis and miscellaneous unknown casework, and currently also serves as team leader of this combined section.

Ms Hendrikse is very active in the forensic fire debris community in Europe. She has been a member of the Fire & Explosions Investigation Working Group (FEIWG) of the European Network of Forensic Science Institutes (ENFSI) since 2004. As a member of this working group, she has been the driving force in the development and coordination of a European collaborative testing scheme for ignitable liquid analysis in fire debris. She is currently a steering-committee member, and is leading the establishment of a European database of ignitable liquids.

Ms Hendrikse is involved in the training of national fire investigators, and lecturing on the subjects in her field of expertise to members from the Dutch legal system.

Ms Hendrikse holds a Master of Science degree in Analytical Chemistry from Leiden University (the Netherlands). Before becoming a forensic scientist at the NFI, she worked as a chemist at the international Organization for the Prohibition of Chemical Weapons (OPCW) in The Hague for 7 years, the industrial company Hoechst Holland in Vlissingen for 1 year, the printing office Lawson Mardon in Bergen op Zoom for 1 year, and the environmental laboratory SGS Ecocare in 's-Gravenpolder for 2 years (all located in the Netherlands).

Michiel M.P. Grutters, PhD

Michiel Grutters is a forensic scientist at the Netherlands Forensic Institute (NFI) in The Hague, the Netherlands, a position he has held since 2010. He is a forensic expert in the area of fire debris analysis.

He is the author of over 750 case reports in fire debris analysis. He has been involved in the education of national fire investigators and students at both bachelor and master's level.

Michiel Grutters obtained his MSc degree in chemistry from Utrecht University (the Netherlands). He performed his PhD research at Eindhoven University of Technology (the Netherlands) in the field of homogenous catalysis under supervision of Prof. Dr D. Vogt. Prior to joining the NFI, he worked for 5 years in the area of food analysis at the Food and Consumer Product Safety Authority in Eindhoven (the Netherlands).

Frank A.M. Schäfer, PhD

Since 1995 Frank Schäfer has been employed as a forensic scientist at the Forensic Institute of the German Federal Criminal Police Office (Bundeskriminalamt, "BKA"). A forensic expert in the areas of fire debris analysis and fire scene examination, he also acts as a forensic contact person for cases involving radio nuclear material. His experience includes serving with the Drug Section of the BKA, where he was responsible for a Research and Development programme.

His current position is as deputy leader of the fire section of the BKA Forensic Science Institute.

Frank Schäfer received his diploma in chemistry and his doctoral degree in nuclear and analytical chemistry from the Johannes-Gutenberg-University of Mainz (Germany).

INTRODUCTION

The following Guideline for Identifying Ignitable Liquids in Fire Debris is an addition to the ASTM E1618 "Standard Test Method for Ignitable Liquid Residues in Extracts from Fire Debris Samples by Gas Chromatography-Mass Spectrometry" [1]. The ASTM E1618 is accepted as a base document. This guideline provides more detail when it comes to the identification of the different classes of ignitable liquids, as defined by the ASTM.

The overall composition of each product class, and the variation in composition within these classes is discussed and illustrated with examples. Several effects that can distort the composition are addressed as well, such as evaporation, microbial degradation, and interference of pyrolysis products. Finally, the characteristics of each product class that are considered necessary for identification are listed.

The range of both ignitable liquid products and substrates containing an ignitable liquid as an ingredient on the market is huge. An in-house, up-to-date reference collection is of utmost importance to maintain the greatest possible overview on the production and composition of these products and substrates, in addition to what can be found in the scientific literature and other sources (e.g., [2,3]).

CHAPTER 1

Ignitable Liquid Products

The term "ignitable liquid" is a common term in fire investigation. It is a frequently used term in handbooks and scientific literature related to fire debris analysis without being further defined. The only definition for "ignitable liquid" is found in NFPA® 921, "Guide for Fire and Explosion Investigations" [4], where it is defined as: "Any liquid or the liquid phase of any material that is capable of fueling a fire, including a flammable liquid, combustible liquid, or any other material that can be liquefied and burned". This indicates that it is an umbrella term for all sorts of flammable and combustible liquids, which can be involved in the initiation or development of a fire.

The definition by NFPA® 921 involves all flammable and combustible liquids without flash point limitations. A particular category of these, however, cannot be recovered with the fire debris analysis methods commonly employed. These methods are based on the gas chromatographic analysis of the (heated) headspace of the debris samples instead of the analysis of the debris materials themselves.

Common fire debris analysis methods are generally limited to the recovery of flammable and combustible liquids up to a flash point of approximately 100 °C[1]. Combustible liquids with a higher or no flash point will not be recovered[2]. Such liquids will in particular intensify a fire, but will not usually easily initiate a fire. Although this category of liquids is considered to be of less interest in relation to fire cause investigation, for reasons of clarity it is important that the range of liquids that is covered by the analysis is defined.

Ignitable liquids with a flash point up to 93 °C are categorized by the Globally Harmonized System of Classification and Labeling of Chemicals (GHS) based on their flash point and for some categories

---

[1] The upper flash point limit depends on the heating conditions of the method employed.
[2] Such liquids are, for example, lubricant and olive oil.

Table 1.1 Ignitable Liquid Classification According to GHS		
Category	Criteria	Classification
1	Flash point <23 °C and initial boiling point ≤35 °C	Extremely flammable
2	Flash point <23 °C and initial boiling point >35 °C	Highly flammable
3	Flash point ≥ 23 °C and ≤60 °C	Flammable
4	Flash point >60 °C and ≤93 °C	Combustible

based on their initial boiling point [5]. The GHS categories are outlined in Table 1.1.

In fire debris, the presence of residues of an ignitable liquid can, however, not be determined via a flash point analysis. Instead, it is identified through its chemical composition, commonly via the analysis of the (heated) headspace of the sample. For the purpose of fire debris analysis ignitable liquids are therefore classified based on their chemical composition. An example of such a classification is included in ASTM E1618. Although the term "ignitable liquid" in ASTM E1618 is not defined, it can be deducted from the examples in its classification scheme that it includes flammable and combustible liquids with a flash point up to approximately 100 °C.

CHAPTER 2

ASTM E1618

2.1 INTRODUCTION

ASTM E1618 "Standard Test Method for Ignitable Liquid Residues in Extracts from Fire Debris Samples by Gas Chromatography-Mass Spectrometry" [1] describes a general GCMS-method for the analysis of ignitable liquids in fire debris samples, and guidelines for the interpretation of the analysis results. It includes an ignitable liquid classification scheme and minimum identification criteria for each of the defined product classes. In addition, it provides comments and warnings that may be important in the interpretation process of the fire debris analysis results.

2.2 ASTM E1618 CLASSIFICATION SCHEME

The ASTM E1618 classification scheme includes seven major classes of ignitable liquid compositions:

- Gasoline (all brands, including gasohol and E85)
- Petroleum Distillates (including De-Aromatized)
- Isoparaffinic Products
- Aromatic Products
- Naphthenic-Paraffinic Products
- Normal Alkane Products
- Oxygenated Solvents.

In addition, it includes a class Other-Miscellaneous for those product compositions which either do not fall into one of the above listed classes, or which fall into more than one of the above listed classes.

The classes, except for the gasoline class, are divided into three subclasses based on boiling (*n*-alkane) range:

- Light product range (n-C_4–n-C_9)
- Medium product range (n-C_8–n-C_{13})
- Heavy product range (n-C_9–n-C_{20+}).

Identifying Ignitable Liquids in Fire Debris.

In addition to composition based, Gasoline is defined as a separate class because of its specific application and Petroleum Distillates because of their origin ("straight-run" fractions of crude oil). All the other classes are solely defined by chemical composition because both the applications and production processes of the products within these classes can be diverse. The same chemical composition may for example be used/sold both as lamp oil and as a solvent for insecticides. They may be produced from crude oil or by a synthetic process. When produced from crude oil, they will have undergone further refinement and/or treatment, and as a result will have lost too many of the crude oil characteristics for classification as Petroleum Distillate.

2.3 ASTM E1618 MINIMUM IDENTIFICATION CRITERIA

The minimum identification criteria of each product class are not strict. They leave enough room for the fact that the chemical composition of products within each of these classes may (slightly) vary from product to product, and from product batch to product batch, and may be influenced by external factors such as evaporation (e.g., due to the heat of the fire) and microbial degradation (due to the presence of bacteria and/or fungi).

As an example, the minimum criteria for the identification of gasoline in ASTM E1618-14 include: "Aromatics—Petroleum pattern comparable to that of the reference ignitable liquids" and "Alkanes— Present. Pattern may vary by brand, grade, and lot".

The intent of ASTM E1618 is to allow ignitable liquids to be characterized as belonging to one of the classes in the classification scheme and to provide a means for harmonization in classification between fire debris experts from different laboratories, countries, and continents. However, it must be noted that due to the wide variety of ignitable liquid products available and on-going development, changes, and innovations in production processes there will always be products with a chemical composition for which it is difficult to identify the correct product class. According to ASTM E1618, these compositions should be classified as Other-Miscellaneous. In practice, this often leads to different classifications of the same product amongst fire debris experts and is food for discussion.

2.4 ASTM E1618 VERSUS GUIDELINE

The current guideline elaborates on ASTM E1618 and offers an additional means to promote harmonization of the classification of ignitable liquids. It discusses and illustrates in more detail the (variation in) chemical composition of each defined product class of ignitable liquids. It illustrates the effects that may distort these compositions. For some product classes it provides additional characteristics for identification purposes, which could in particular be helpful in situations of doubt.

CHAPTER 3

General Production Processes of Ignitable Liquid Products

3.1 INTRODUCTION

Ignitable liquid products are derived from crude oil or are produced synthetically, for example, from carbon-based feedstock such as natural gas, coal, or biomass. This chapter provides general background information on the production of both crude oil and noncrude oil based products.

3.2 CRUDE OIL FUELS

Today, crude oil (also known as petroleum) is still the main feedstock for engine and heating fuels and also an invaluable feedstock for the chemical industry. These days, many commonly used products, from plastics to pharmaceuticals, are based on crude oil, including many ignitable liquid products.

3.2.1 Petroleum Refinery

Crude oil is a fossil fuel, a natural product of decaying plants and animals that lived in ancient seas millions of years ago. It consists of a complex mixture of hydrocarbons, mostly alkanes (paraffins), cycloalkanes (naphthenes), and aromatic hydrocarbons. More complex compounds such as asphalthenes are present as well. The exact composition of crude oil varies widely. Generally, the hydrocarbon composition ranges from C_5 to C_{40}.

Crude oil is refined and separated into a large number of intermediate and end products. The main breakdown products from a typical oil refinery are gasoline (approx. 45%), jet fuel (approx. 10%), diesel and other fuels (approx. 25%) [6], but it must be noted that there is a large variation in oil refinery configurations.

Identifying Ignitable Liquids in Fire Debris.

Intermediate products are used for different applications and purposes:

- They are used as a pool for blending of technical products like gasoline.
- They are used as feedstock for the production of basic and special products such as waxes, olefins, aromatics, isoparaffins, and naphthenes (which involve further treatment steps such as desulfurization, hydrogenation, cracking, and isomerization).
- They are sold directly to the (petro-)chemical industry.

3.2.2 Primary Petroleum Distillates

Primary petroleum distillates are crude oil refining fractions from the first refining process, the atmospheric distillation. After a desalting step, the crude oil is separated into different boiling range fractions, such as:

- uncondensable gas,
- light naphtha,
- heavy naphtha,
- kerosene,
- light gasoil,
- heavy gasoil,
- athmospheric residue.

All of these "straight-run" distillates are characterized by dominating alkanes, in particular n-alkanes in a Gaussian-like distribution and branched alkanes and cycloalkanes (naphthenes) in a characteristic crude oil "fingerprint" pattern at relatively low concentrations. Aromatics are present at relatively low level too. The higher boiling range fractions include isoprenoïds, which are typical biomarkers from crude oil, at fingerprint level as well.

Before becoming available as an end product they undergo some further treatment, mostly to remove sulfur-compounds and nitrogen-compounds.

3.2.2.1 Naphtha

Naphtha is a very important distillation fraction in the petrochemical industry. It is an important blending fraction in the production of motor gasoline, an important feedstock in the production of special solvents for the chemical and pharmaceutical industry and also for a wide range of household products (such as stain remover, brass polish, roof primer).

For the latter application naphtha is often narrowed down in boiling range by further distillation steps, even down to single compounds.

Because of the high petrochemical value of "straight-run" naphtha a secondary stream of naphtha is produced from raw or refined products by the cracking processes.

3.2.2.2 Kerosene

Kerosene is an important distillation fraction for a variety of products. The boiling range may vary, depending on the distillation process employed and on the product specification set. It may be treated to meet the required product specifications.

Applications of kerosene are:

*   Lamp kerosene, nowadays with specifications for smoke point, flash point, and volatility.
*   Cleaning, defatting, and industrial solvents.
*   Jet fuels, with an extensive set of stringent specifications (Table 3.1).

3.2.2.3 Gasoil

Gasoil has a boiling range of approximately 170–360 °C. The end product is however often a blend product of both "straight-run" gasoil and gasoil from the second distillation process, the vacuum distillation[1]. The composition still resembles that of crude oil, but the

Table 3.1 Major Civil Jet Fuel Grades and Their Specification[a]		
Grade	Area of Usage	Major Specification
Jet A-1	World-wide	ASTM D1655, DEF STAN 91-91 (DERD 2494)
Jet A	USA only	ASTM D 1655
TS-1	Russia and former Eastern Bloc countries	GOST 10227
Jet Fuel no.3	China	GB 6537
Jet A-1	Canada	CAN/CGSB-3.23
[a]Bishop (2011). Aviation turbine fuels. Ullmann's Encyclopedia of Industrial Chemistry.		

---

[1] Other streams may be blended as well, such as paraffins from FT-synthesis (XTL-products like GTL, BTL, CTL) or from hydrotreatment (e.g., from hydrotreated vegetable oils, HVOs). Recycled products from used oils are not allowed.

Gaussian-like distribution of the main components may be (heavily) distorted as a result of this blending.

Gasoil is mainly used as diesel fuel and domestic heating fuel. For both applications a large range of additives[2] is added, ensuring stability over time and stable performance under varying operation conditions. For tax purposes heating fuel is dyed in some countries.

Diesel fuel may contain fatty acid esters (typically methyl esters, FAMEs), to meet the European Directive on biofuels [7].

The specifications of diesel fuel in Europe are fixed in EN 590 (Automotive fuels—Diesel—Requirements and test methods) [8] and include mostly physical parameters. The most significant changes in requirements in the last 20 years are the reduction of sulfur content and the introduction of fatty acid esters up to approximately 7% (v/v) in 2014. The necessity to reduce the content of aromatic compounds has been discussed in the literature, but has not yet been implemented in the relevant standards (except for polycyclic aromatic hydrocarbons).

For domestic heating fuel only national standards are available, for example, the German standard DIN 51603-1.

3.2.3 Gasoline

Gasoline is an important refinery blend product of crude oil. Historically it was produced from the naphtha-fraction. Nowadays, most, if not all, refineries also convert other fractions to increase the yield of gasoline and meet the increasing demand for it. As a result gasoline is now a complex blend from different refinery processes. These processes involve chemical conversion and reformulation processes such as high vacuum distillation, catalytic and thermal cracking, catalytic reforming, isomerization, alkylation, and treatment processes such as hydrotreatment. The processes employed, however, can vary from refinery to refinery and depend on both the variety of processes available and on the demand/quantity of gasoline and other refinery products.

After the various gasoline streams have been blended, additives and blending agents are added to improve the performance and stability of

---

[2] For example, nitrates, one of which is ethylhexylnitrate, for ignition and cetane improvement.

gasoline. These compounds include antiknock agents, antioxidants, metal deactivators, lead scavengers, antirust agents, anti-icing agents, etc.

At the end of the refining process the gasoline end product is a complex mixture of hydrocarbons, which is mainly defined by its physical properties such as vapor pressure, Research Octane Number, and Motor Octane Number. Although the chemical composition of gasoline is not defined, it proves to be a combination of alkanes (C_4-C_{12}), aromatics (alkylbenzenes, indanes, naphthalenes), and oxygenates (such as ethanol and ethers like methyl tert-butyl ether [MTBE] and ethyl tert-butyl ether [ETBE]) in the boiling range of approximately 35–200 °C. The exact chemical composition of gasoline, however, varies from refinery to refinery and from batch to batch within the same refinery, because it is determined by the composition of the crude oil, and the refinery and blending processes employed. These processes may change over time within a refinery, depending on the demand and costs for gasoline and other refinery products.

The specifications of gasoline in Europe are fixed in EN 228 (Automotive fuels—Unleaded petrol—Requirements and test methods) [9] and include mostly physical parameters. The most significant changes in requirements in the last 20 years are the reduction of sulfur content, the benzene content, the content of other aromatics, and the introduction of oxygenated compounds.

3.3 NONCRUDE OIL FUELS

Due to the imminent depletion of oil and the effect its usage has on the environment[3]. research for alternatives is ongoing. Especially since 2000, research and development has focused on replacing the crude oil feedstock essential for today's life.

The intensified use of natural gas and coal are only temporary solutions because they are hampered by the same disadvantages as crude oil. For that reason extensive development is ongoing in exploring and producing alternatives from other sources, such as biomass.

---

[3] Greenhouse gas effect, that is, CO_2 -source.

The following paragraphs shortly describe the main alternative processes, which have been developed or are under development, to give the reader an idea of the current possibilities.

3.3.1 XTL-Fuel

XTL-fuels [10] are synthetic liquid fuels, produced through specialized conversion processes of carbon-based feedstock, such as coal, natural gas, or biomass. The X in XTL stands for the source material used:

- CTL: Coal-To-Liquid
- GTL: Gas-To-Liquid
- BTL: Biomass-To-Liquid.

3.3.1.1 Coal-To-Liquid

Coal can be converted directly or indirectly into liquids. It is converted directly through liquefaction (via hydrogenation or pyrolysis and carbonization processes): this is done by breaking down the organic coal structure by the application of solvents or catalysts in a high pressure and temperature environment. It is converted indirectly by converting the coal into synthesis gas[4] first and subsequently converting[5] this gas into new hydrocarbons, which act as feedstock in the refinery for the refinement of new liquid fuels, such as diesel fuel. The indirect conversion is commercially more favorable than the direct liquefaction. It is used in different plants over the world.

Indirect conversion includes three steps that occur in the presence of catalysts:

1. **Syngas Formation**:
   Old Hydrocarbon + Oxygen → Syngas
2. **Fischer-Tropsch (FT) Reaction**:
   Syngas → New Hydrocarbon + Water
3. **Refining**:
   New Hydrocarbon → Fuels, Chemicals, etc.

The FT-process involves a series of chemical reactions that produce a variety of hydrocarbons. These hydrocarbons are mostly *n*-alkanes, but as a result of competing reactions also (smaller amounts of) branched   alkanes,   alkenes,   alcohols,   and   other   oxygenated

---

[4] Synthesis gas, also referred to as "syngas", is a purified mixture of CO and H_2 gas.
[5] Via the FT-process.

compounds can be formed. The FT-reaction products depend on the FT-conditions employed. The High-Temperature FT-Process mainly produces short-chain end products, which are mainly used as feedstock for the chemical industry, and gasoline and diesel production. The Low-Temperature FT-Process mainly produces longer chain end product, mainly used as feedstock for the production of diesel fuel and wax.

3.3.1.2 Gas-To-Liquid

Natural gas can be converted into liquids, also via the FT-process as described above. Some refineries have brought GTL fluids and solvents on the market, as, for example, GTL-diesel, lamp oil, and lighter fluid [11,12].

GTL-diesel is sold as such, as well as blended into the conventional diesel fuel obtained from the refinement of crude oil. Compared to conventional diesel fuel, GTL-diesel does not contain isoprenoïds, cycloalkanes, or aromatics. Due to the absence of aromatics, it is considered a more environmentally friendly fuel. An example of a total ion current (TIC) chromatogram of a GTL-diesel versus a conventional diesel fuel is illustrated in Figure 3.1; a description of the method conditions employed is summarized in Annex A. The comparison of GTL-diesel versus conventional diesel fuel is further discussed in paragraph 6.3.4.5.

3.3.1.3 Biomass-To-Liquid

Biomass can be converted into liquid biofuels through a thermochemical route. The biomass is pretreated and then converted to syngas via gasification. The resulting syngas is then cleaned prior to conversion to liquid biofuels, mostly by FT-synthesis.

The scope of BTL is to convert waste biomass, for example, from the processing of wood, corn, sugar, or other agricultural waste, into high quality liquid fuels. This avoids concurrency with food production and offers an additional yield from its waste—two advantages, both from the ethical and economical point of view.

3.3.2 Biomass-Based Fuels

Biomass as a source for new fuels for engine and heating means is drawing increasing attention because of the fact that the end of fossil

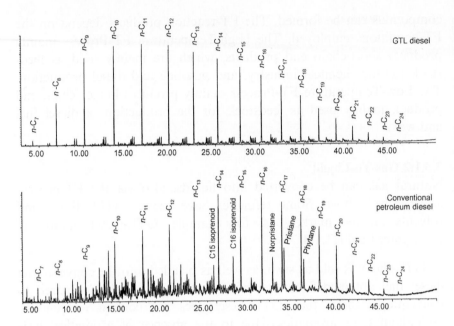

Figure 3.1 TICs of GTL-diesel and conventional petroleum diesel (GCMS of pentane dilution).

fuels is getting near. Increasing use of biofuels also helps to reduce the rising energy costs, to improve energy security, and to address global warming concerns.

Biofuels [13] can be separated into three "generations", based on the timescale of their research and marketing:

- first generation biofuels,
- second generation biofuels,
- third generation biofuels.

Between generations, the composition of the biofuels themselves does not change, but rather the source from which the fuels are derived.

The most important biofuels are:

- Bioethanol, obtained through fermentation of sugars and biomass.
- Biodiesel, obtained through esterification of vegetable oils.
- Renewable diesel, obtained through hydrotreating of vegetable oils[6].

---

[6] Known as the HVO process, such as the NExBTL-Process from NesteOil.

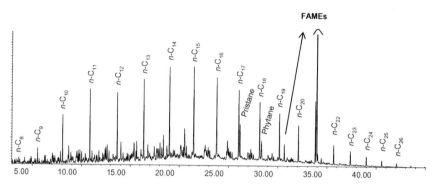

Figure 3.2 TIC of diesel fuel with addition of FAME (GCMS, direct injection).

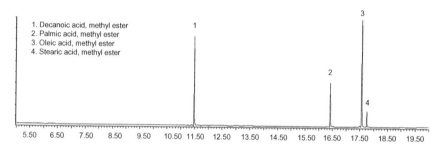

Figure 3.3 FAME as ignitable liquid on a white BBQ-lighter (GCMS of isooctane extract).

Bioethanol is used as a blend component in gasoline as such, and used as starting material for the production of other oxygenated gasoline additives, such as bio-ETBE.

Biodiesel consists of fatty acid esters (typically FAMEs). It is used both as a blend fraction in conventional diesel fuel, and in some countries as a 100% alternative fuel for conventional diesel fuel[7]. An example of diesel fuel with biodiesel is illustrated in Figure 3.2.

Fatty acid esters are also used as technical solvents in commercial products, such as white barbeque lighter blocks. The FAME composition in these blocks is illustrated in Figure 3.3; a description of the method conditions employed is summarized in Annex A.

3.3.2.1 First Generation Biofuels [13]

First generation biofuels are primarily made from the edible portions of food crops. Examples include sugar cane, corn, and wheat.

[7] Only possible after adjustment of the engine.

Except for HVOs, first generation fuels cannot be used as a direct replacement of fossil fuels without precautions (without modifications to the engine). Instead, they are blended with fossil fuels to reduce the usage of fossil fuels.

The high costs of production, competition with food, low land-use efficiency, modest greenhouse gas emission reduction, and the many unused by-products (such as plant waste, glycerol, etc.) have led to extensive research into new pathways for synthetic production of fuels.

3.3.2.2 Second Generation Biofuels [13]
Second generation biofuels are fuels obtained from various types of biomass which are not related to food. Second generation biofuels are made from plants that are grown for this purpose (energy crops) or from inedible parts of food crops, such as straw, woodchips, and used cooking oil.

3.3.2.3 Third Generation Biofuels [13]
Third generation biofuels are obtained from feedstock that is capable of producing high biofuel yields from rather low resource inputs, compared to the other sources from which first and second generation biofuels are obtained. Examples of these are:

- "Designer"-oil seeds with enhanced yield.
- Plants, especially trees with lower lignin content and higher growth rates.
- Algae and microorganisms.

Research on the production of third generation biofuels is ongoing.

CHAPTER *4*

Fire Debris Analysis Methods

4.1 INTRODUCTION

The most commonly used method for the analysis of ignitable liquid residues in fire debris samples is heated headspace sampling followed by GCMS analysis. The headspace can either be sampled directly, called static headspace sampling, or via an adsorbent, called passive or dynamic headspace sampling. Typical adsorbents used are activated charcoal, Tenax®, and SPME-fibers.

Other extraction methods are distillation and solvent extraction. The distillation method is seldom used because it is too cumbersome and time-consuming. The solvent extraction method is still in use in some laboratories, mostly as a confirmation method or as a method to distinguish between medium and heavy petroleum distillates [14,15].

General procedures for the different methods can be found in the literature [16–20]. They can be used as the starting point for the development and validation of an in-house method.

4.2 ADVANTAGES AND DISADVANTAGES OF EXTRACTION METHODS

Each extraction method has its advantages and drawbacks. Among the different headspace sampling methods, the direct sampling is the simplest and fastest but the least sensitive. The dynamic sampling method is most sensitive but the most time-consuming. Many laboratories employ the "medium sensitive" passive headspace sampling method—mostly by placing the adsorbent for a certain time in the headspace, or by extracting a certain volume of the headspace through the adsorbent with a syringe. Figure 4.1 shows the total ion current (TIC) chromatograms of a gasoline–diesel oil (1:2) mixture obtained via different modes of operation: static heated headspace, preconcentrated heated

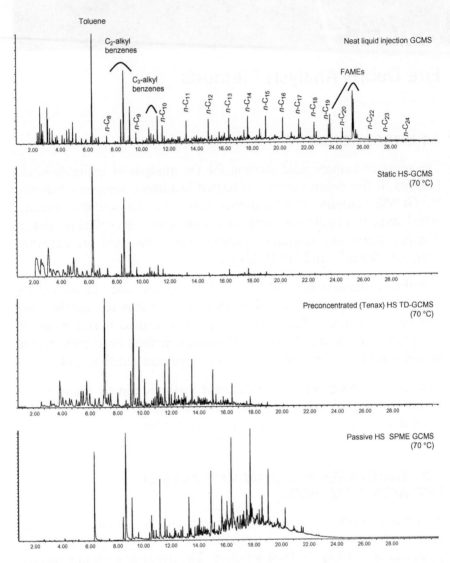

Figure 4.1 Effect of extraction method on the recovery of a gasoline–diesel oil mixture (1:2): neat liquid injection GCMS, static HS-GCMS 1, HS Tenax® TD-GCMS, and passive HS CAR-PDMS SPME GCMS.

headspace on Tenax®, and passive heated headspace on a 75 μm CAR-PDMS SPME fiber. The result of a neat liquid injection is illustrated as reference. A description of the different method conditions employed is summarized in Annex A. The chromatograms are normalized to the component with highest intensity.

4.3 INFLUENCES ON RECOVERY OF IGNITABLE LIQUID COMPOSITIONS

Factors that may have an influence on the recovery of the ignitable liquid residue composition when headspace sampling is employed, are:

- the headspace analysis method employed (static, passive, dynamic)
- the headspace temperature and the sampling temperature
- the headspace extraction time/volume, sampled on the adsorbent
- the type of adsorbent used for sampling (if used)
- the adsorption capacity of the adsorbent used for sampling (if used)
- the ignitable liquid concentration present in the fire debris sample.

The effects of headspace temperature, sampling time/volume, and ignitable liquid concentration are illustrated in Figures 4.2–4.4, respectively[1].

4.3.1 Effect of Headspace Temperature

At elevated temperatures, the recovery of volatiles from the sample is increased. In particular the recovery of the least volatile components. Care must be taken when the sample is heated above 100 °C, because at this temperature (extinguishing) water vaporizes as well. The effect of sample temperature on the recovery of a gasoline–diesel oil mixture (1:2) with heated headspace on Tenax® followed by TD-GCMS analysis is illustrated in Figure 4.2.

4.3.2 Effect of Sampling Time/Volume

The recovery of the least volatile components will be improved by increasing sampling time/volume. However, too long sampling times or too large sampling volumes may result in displacement of volatiles when the capacity of the adsorbent is reached. The effect of sampling time on the recovery of a gasoline–diesel oil mixture (1:2) with passive heated (70 °C) headspace sampling on a 100 μm PDMS SPME-fiber is illustrated in Figure 4.3.

---

[1] Method conditions are summarized in Annex A, and chromatograms (TICs) are normalized to the highest peak.

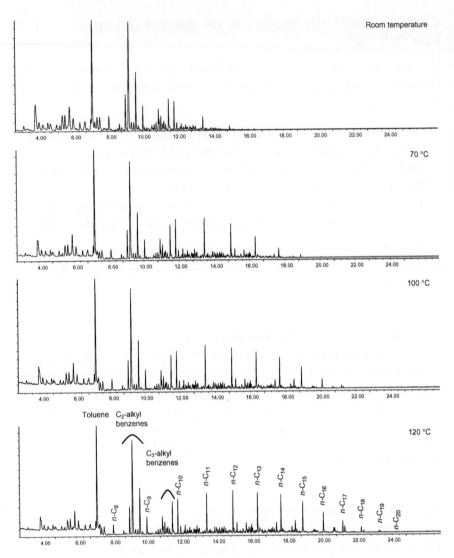

Figure 4.2 Effect of headspace temperature on the recovery of a gasoline–diesel oil mixture (1:2), with headspace sampling on Tenax® followed by TD-GCMS.

Note that the *y*-scales of the chromatograms in Figure 4.3 differ greatly because the recovery of volatiles after 15 min sampling is much higher than the recovery after 1 min and 5 s sampling.

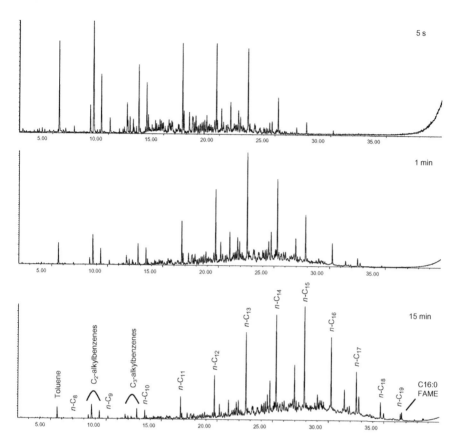

Figure 4.3 Effect of sampling time on the recovery of a gasoline–diesel oil mixture (1:2), with passive headspace sampling on a PDMS fiber followed by GCMS.

4.3.3 Effect of Ignitable Liquid Concentration

The recovery of the ignitable liquid composition by the headspace method depends on the concentration of the ignitable liquid present in the fire debris sample. Figure 4.4 illustrates that as the amount of ignitable liquid in the sample container (i.e., 2.5 L glass jar) increases, the relative concentration of the more volatile components of the ignitable liquid in the gas phase increases accordingly.

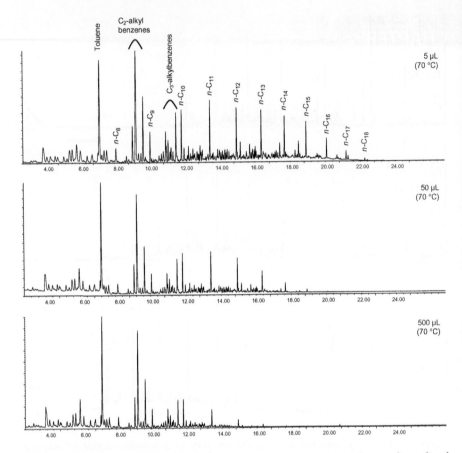

Figure 4.4 Effect of ignitable liquid concentration on the recovery of a gasoline–diesel mixture (1:2) with headspace sampling on Tenax® followed by TD-GCMS.

It is important for the chemist to know the limitations of the methods employed for recovery and analysis. This reduces the risk of false positive identifications and/or erroneous classifications during the interpretation of the analysis results obtained. The parameters of the method(s) employed must be selected in such a way that the characteristics, listed in this document for each ASTM E1618 product class, can be identified.

CHAPTER 5

Interferences in Identification of Ignitable Liquid Products

5.1 INTRODUCTION

Interfering products in fire debris samples are defined as (a combination of) compounds that interfere with either the correct identification of ignitable liquid residues or with the correct determination of the evidential value of the identified residues in relation to the possible cause of the fire [21]. The sources of these interfering products fall into two main categories:

- Substrate background products (present on/in the substrate prior to the fire).
- Pyrolysis and combustion products (formed and released during the heating, burning, and pyrolysis of the substrate).

It is important for the fire debris expert to have a wide and up-to-date knowledge of the composition and manufacturing processes of substrate materials that can be found at a fire scene. This knowledge can be obtained from literature and from the analysis of a collection of different substrate products and materials (e.g., household products, polymers), both nonburned and burned/pyrolyzed (e.g. [22]).

The following paragraphs give some examples of substrate background products and some basic information on pyrolysis and combustion products which are released from substrate materials that are commonly found at fire scenes and often submitted for fire debris analysis. Amongst others these include flooring materials, wood, paper, fabric, polymers, building materials, and soil [23–25].

5.2 SUBSTRATE BACKGROUND PRODUCTS

Substrate background products, such as individual compounds, solvents, distillates, etc., are present on/in the substrate prior to the fire. These background products may either be part of the natural substrate due to manufacturing processes, or contamination of the samples from, for example, household cleaners, adhesives, and treatment products.

In some substrate materials the ignitable liquid is ignitable at ambient temperatures, whereas in others it is not, dependent on concentration. From the results of a regular headspace analysis, the origin[1] of the identified ignitable liquid volatiles can often not be determined. It is therefore important to report on the ignitable liquid residues, together with examples of trade names of pure liquids and of substrate materials in which such a liquid can be present. Providing these examples may help in determining the evidential value of the fire debris analysis findings, in particular, when this interpretation is done by any other person than the fire debris expert.

Examples of typical substrate background materials with an ignitable liquid as an ingredient are summarized in Table 5.1. More examples can be found in the literature [1,26−28].

Table 5.1 Examples of Typical Background Products Found in Substrates in the Netherlands	
ASTM E1618 Class	Examples of Substrate Background Materials
Gasoline—all brands, including gasohol and E85	–
Petroleum Distillates (including De-Aromatized)	Some roof repair pastes/glues, some glues, copper polish, some shoe polish, some furniture cleaners/waxes, some wax removers, some paints, some printing inks, some penetrating oils, some industrial hand soaps
Isoparaffinic Products	Some glue/kit removers, some stain removers, some furniture cleaners/waxes
Aromatic Products	Some carburetor cleaners, some industrial hand soaps, some paint-brush cleaners, some stain removers, some metal degreasers
Naphthenic-Paraffinic Products	Some stain removers, some correction fluids, some glues/kits
Normal Alkane Products	Some carbonless forms, some matches, polyethylene material
Oxygenated Solvents	Alcoholic drinks, eau de toilettes, perfumes, windscreen washers, some stain removers, coolants, some steel polishers, some detergents, some cleaning agents, some glues
Other-Miscellaneous	Some stain removers, some glues/kits, some furniture cleaners/waxes, some roof repair pastes/glues, soft wood, some correction fluids, some industrial hand soaps

[1] From pure ignitable liquid, or from ignitable liquid residues present in a substrate background product (possibly in an ignitable state, but not necessarily).

5.3 PYROLYSIS AND COMBUSTION PRODUCTS

Pyrolysis and combustion products are formed from the substrates and released during the fire. They can account for a wide range of compounds depending on the nature of the substrate material, the temperature of the fire, the availability of oxygen, etc. The most frequently occurring pyrolysis products are aromatics (such as benzene, toluene, and higher n-alkylbenzenes, naphthalenes, styrenes), alkenes, and n-alkanes in combination with n-alkenes.

Indicators for the presence of pyrolysis products are, for example, high intensities of [29]:

- benzene, often in combination with high intensities of toluene, ethylbenzene, and higher n-alkylbenzenes (products of polyvinyl-based substrates such as polyvinyl chloride and polyvinyl acetate).
- styrene, often in combination with α-methylstyrene and benzene, toluene, ethylbenzene (products of polystyrene based substrates).
- 2,4-dimethylheptene, often in combination with C_{12}- and C_{15}-alkenes (products of polypropylene based substrates).
- n-alkane—n-alkene doublets, sometimes in combination with aldehydes and alkadienes (products of polyethylene based substrates).

The presence of pyrolysis and combustion products may complicate the interpretation of a fire debris analysis result. In particular, when their presence is dominant and/or overlaps with compounds of interest. They often distort the chromatographic patterns that are normally observed for ignitable liquid residues. Caution is necessary when pyrolysis products are present, to avoid that some of them are misinterpreted as ignitable liquid residues.

Although the chromatographic patterns of combustion and pyrolysis products may resemble those of ignitable liquids, they can be distinguished. However, relatively small quantities of ignitable liquid residues cannot always be easily identified in the predominating presence of pyrolysis products.

Some examples of frequently occurring substrate materials in fire debris are shown in Figures 5.1–5.5. These chromatograms have been obtained from burned/pyrolyzed materials subjected to radiant heat. The chromatograms give an example of the volatiles to be expected

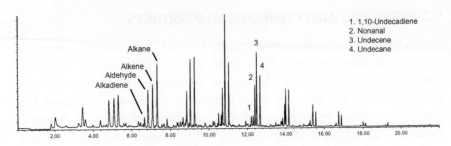

Figure 5.1 TIC of burned/pyrolyzed high density polyethylene (TD-GCMS).

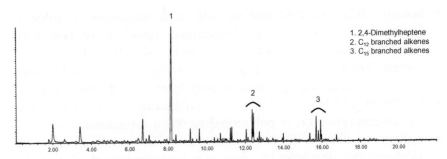

Figure 5.2 TIC of burned/pyrolyzed polypropylene (TD-GCMS).

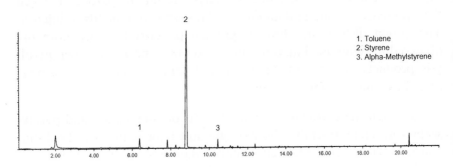

Figure 5.3 TIC of burned/pyrolyzed polystyrene (TD-GCMS).

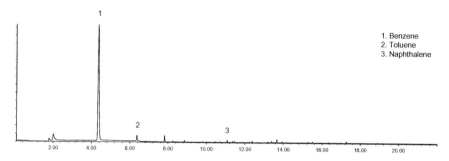

Figure 5.4 TIC of burned/pyrolyzed polyvinyl chloride (TD-GCMS).

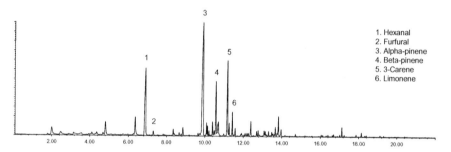

Figure 5.5 TIC of burned/pyrolyzed soft wood (TD-GCMS).

from these materials after burning/pyrolysis. The exact composition of volatiles, however, depends on the conditions of the fire.

A description of the GCMS method conditions employed is given in Annex A. The chromatograms are normalized to the component with highest intensity.

CHAPTER 6

Guidance for Identifying Ignitable Liquids in Fire Debris

6.1 INTRODUCTION

This chapter outlines the characteristics and variation in composition of the different ignitable liquid classes defined by ASTM E1618. For each class the following is described and illustrated:

- the overall composition;
- the variation in composition;
- the effects that can influence the composition (such as evaporation, microbial degradation, and matrix interference/pyrolysis);
- the characteristics in composition which should be demonstrated for a positive identification (these elaborate on the minimum identification criteria defined by ASTM E1618 and are supplemented by supportive criteria suggestions for some product classes).

In general, the compounds of interest in ignitable liquid analysis can be grouped into three families: aromatics, alkanes, and oxygenates. Each family with corresponding compounds or compound groups and their corresponding fragment ions are listed in Table 6.1. The presence or absence of these compound families varies with each ignitable liquid class.

In evaluating the fire debris analysis results:

- the presence or absence of at least all of the compound families listed in Table 6.1 should be considered;
- the presence or absence of compounds characteristic of pyrolysis and/or combustion, such as alkenes, must be considered;
- the concentration ratios within and between the compound families will have to be reviewed, if compounds from one or more of the listed families are present.

Identifying Ignitable Liquids in Fire Debris.

Table 6.1 Ignitable Liquid Compound Families with Corresponding Fragment Ions

Compound Family	(Group of) Compound(s)	Fragment Ion(s) (*m/z*)
Alkanes	*n*-Alkanes, branched alkanes	43, 57, 71, 85, ...
	Cycloalkanes	41, 55, 69, 83, 97, ...[a]
Aromatics	Toluene	91
	C$_2$-Alkylbenzenes	91, 106
	C$_3$-Alkylbenzenes	91, 105, 120
	C$_4$-Alkylbenzenes	91, 119, 134
	Indane	117
	Methylindanes	117, 132
	Naphthalene	128
	Methylnaphthalenes	142
Oxygenates	Alcohols	31, 45, 59, ...
	Ketones	43, 58, 72, 86, ...
	Acetates	43
	Ethers	
	Methyl-tert-butylether (MTBE)	57, 73
	Ethyl-tert-butylether (ETBE)	59, 87
	Tert-amyl-methylether (TAME)	55, 73, 87
	Tert-amyl-ethylether (TAEE)	59, 73, 87
	Methyl esters of fatty acids (FAMEs)	
	Saturated FAMEs	74, 87
	Single unsaturated FAMEs	55, 74, 87
	Double unsaturated FAMEs	55, 67

[a]*Note that cycloalkanes and alkenes share the same fragment ions, but can be differentiated based on retention time and mass spectra.*

Note. The majority of the chromatograms illustrated in the following paragraphs have been obtained by thermal desorption (TD) GCMS analysis from preconcentrated heated (70 °C) headspace on Tenax®. A second group has been generated by direct heated (70 °C) headspace GCMS analysis to better illustrate the composition of very volatile and/or short-chain oxygenated components. A third group has been produced by liquid injection to better illustrate the full boiling range of the products. A description of the different method conditions employed is summarized in Annex A. The chromatograms are normalized to the component with highest intensity.

6.2 GASOLINE

6.2.1 Introduction

The composition of gasoline is defined and controlled by physical properties. Within these specifications the chemical composition of gasoline may vary and depends amongst other factors on the composition of the crude oils used, the refinery processes available/employed, and the overall balance of product demand.

The typical composition of gasoline consists of a combination of alkanes (C_4–C_{12}) and aromatics (alkylbenzenes, indanes, naphthalenes) in the boiling range of approximately 35–200 °C, and often one or more oxygenates (such as ethanol, MTBE, ETBE). A small percentage of alkenes may be present as a result of the refining process. In addition, nonvolatile performance additives may be added to improve the stability and quality of the gasoline. But as these additives are not volatile, and thus not detected by headspace ignitable liquid analysis, they will not be included in the discussion of this document.

6.2.2 Overall Composition of Gasoline

The Total Ion Current (TIC) chromatogram of a common gasoline shows aromatics and branched alkanes as the most abundant components in the boiling range of approximately C_4–C_{12} (depending on the fire debris analysis method employed). A TIC example of a gasoline, obtained by headspace preconcentration on Tenax® and analyzed by TD-GCMS is illustrated in Figure 6.1.

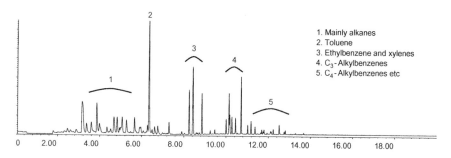

1. Mainly alkanes
2. Toluene
3. Ethylbenzene and xylenes
4. C_3-Alkylbenzenes
5. C_4-Alkylbenzenes etc

Figure 6.1 TIC of common composition of gasoline (TD-GCMS).

The chemical compositions of gasoline can, however, vary because the end product is controlled mostly by physical parameters and not by its chemical composition. Examples of different gasoline compositions are illustrated in Figure 6.7, and additionally can be found in literature [30,31].

For the identification of gasoline, fragment ions of at least the alkanes, aromatics, and oxygenates must be reviewed. An example of Extracted Ion Current (EIC) chromatograms of each of these compound families of a gasoline composition is illustrated in Figure 6.2. Each fragment ion is discussed in more detail in the paragraphs thereafter.

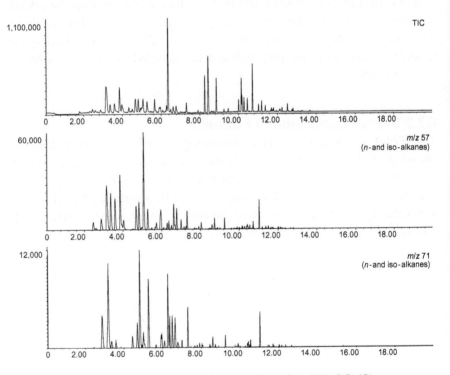

Figure 6.2 TIC and EICs of common composition of gasoline (TD-GCMS).

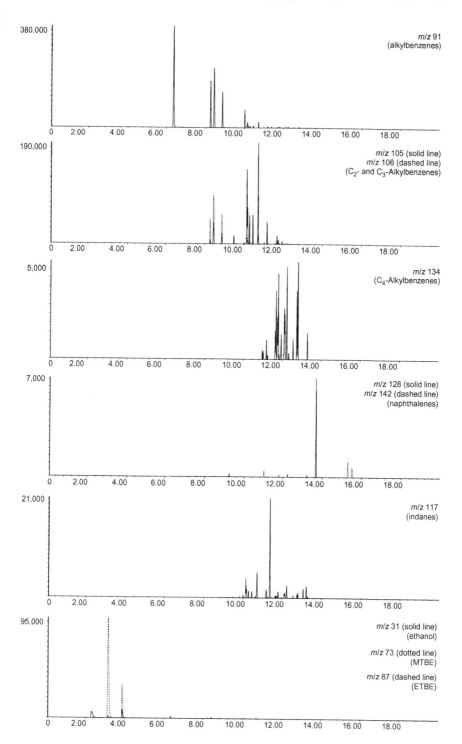

Figure 6.2 (Continued)

When evaluating the presence or absence of alkanes and aromatics, the concentration ratios within and between these groups of compounds must be taken into account as well (within an ion chromatogram and between ion chromatograms). If one or more of these ratios deviate from the ratios of a common gasoline, the following questions will have to be addressed:

- Do the observed ratios occur in reference gasolines (check [own] gasoline database and/or literature)?
- Could the observed ratios be the result of partial evaporation of gasoline?
- Could the observed ratios be the result of microbial degradation?
- Could the observed ratios, or the entire composition be the result of matrix effect (combustion and/or pyrolysis products, selective absorption/adsorption of matrix)?

6.2.2.1 Alkane Composition

The most abundant/important[1] alkanes in an unevaporated gasoline are the C_6- to C_9-alkanes. An example is shown in Figure 6.3. In most gasolines the composition of this alkane fraction is different from that found in crude oil and in "straight-run" light petroleum distillates (LPDs), see Figure 6.4. The alkane fraction in gasoline from modern refineries is often not a straight-run naphtha. Usually, it is a blend of different refinery process-streams such as straight-run naphtha, isomerate, reformate[2], and/or alkylate. The composition of these alkane fractions mainly consists of branched alkanes and can be considered typical for gasoline.

---

[1] The more volatile alkanes (C_4- and C_5-alkanes) can also be abundant, but are difficult to recover from fire debris due to evaporation and the recovery method employed (except for the static HS method).

[2] This aromatic-rich refinery stream can contain alkanes from unreacted feedstock.

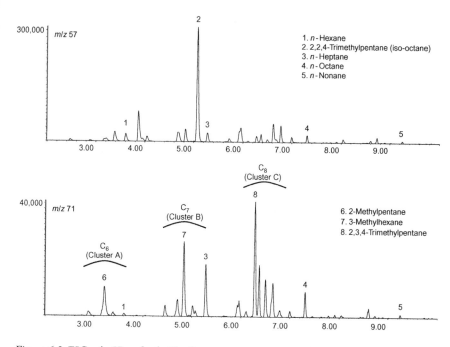

Figure 6.3 EIC m/z *57 and* m/z *71 of common composition of gasoline (TD-GCMS).*

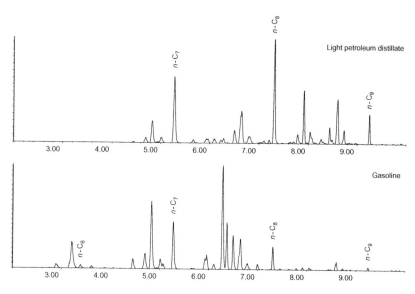

Figure 6.4 EIC m/z *71 of a LPD and a gasoline (TD-GCMS).*

The presence of a dominant cluster of C_8-alkanes (cluster C in Figure 6.3) is mainly the result of the alkylation refinery process. Alkylate is added to gasoline as an octane enhancer. In general, alkylation is the transfer of an alkyl group from one molecule to another. In oil refining it refers to the particular alkylation of isobutane with olefins. Mainly butenes are used, resulting in C_8-alkanes, two of which are isooctane (2,2,4-trimethylpentane), and 2,3,4-trimethylpentane. Propene can also be used resulting in C_7-alkanes, one of which is 2,3-dimethylpentane. [32]

In most gasolines C_6- and C_7-alkanes (cluster A and B in Figure 6.3) are mainly the result of one or more blend streams such as straight-run naphtha and isomerate, and alkanes which may still be present in reformate. In addition, certain C_7-alkanes, one of which is 2,3-dimethylpentane, may originate from alkylate[3]. The composition (pattern) of both the C_6- and C_7-alkanes in most gasolines is different from the composition of the same alkanes in crude oil (and straight-run naphtha): compared to crude oil the intensity of methyl-C_5 versus n-C_6 and/or of methyl-C_6 versus n-C_7 is increased in most gasolines, as can be seen in Figures 6.4 and 6.5.

All of this contributes to the variation of the alkane composition amongst gasolines. In most gasolines from modern refineries the C_6-, C_7-, and C_8-alkane groups (cluster A, B, and C) are present. The variation is reflected both in the intensity ratio between these groups, and in the intensity ratio within these groups (the greatest variation occurring within the C_8-alkane group). Examples of alkane compositions in different gasolines are illustrated in Figure 6.5. Note that the observed alkane patterns may depend on the GC-conditions employed (e.g., column-type and temperature program influence elution order and co-elution of compounds).

---

[3] Note that these are not present in the gasoline example in Figures 6.3 and 6.4.

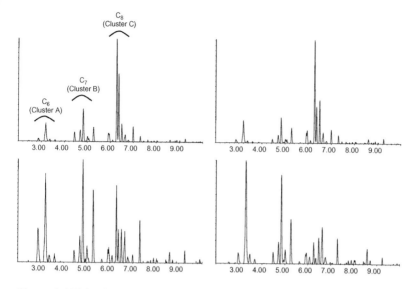

Figure 6.5 EIC m/z 71 of different gasolines (TD-GCMS).

Some gasolines also contain heavier alkanes, usually at a much lower concentration level than the C_6- to C_8-alkane fraction. These heavier alkanes can originate from a diesel oil contamination, as the same transportation equipment (pipelines, trucks, etc.) may be used alternatively for gasoline and diesel oil. Some heavier alkanes, in particular the highly branched C_{12}-alkanes, can originate from the alkylate fraction in the gasoline.

6.2.2.2 Aromatic Composition

The aromatic profile in a common gasoline composition is illustrated in Figure 6.6. Other profiles may be observed, but are less common. Examples of other aromatic profiles are illustrated in Figure 6.7, and can be found in the literature [30,31]. These examples show that the intensity ratios within the C_2-alkylbenzene group and between the C_1-, C_2-, and C_3-alkylbenzene groups can vary.

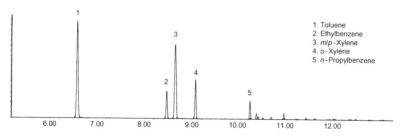

Figure 6.6 EIC m/z 91 of common composition of gasoline (TD-GCMS).

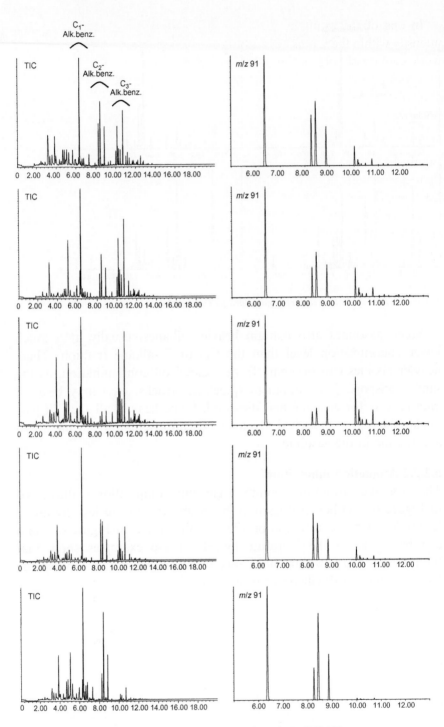

Figure 6.7 TIC and EIC m/z *91 of different gasolines (TD-GCMS).*

In one of the examples in Figure 6.7, ethylbenzene has the highest intensity within the C_2-alkylbenzene group. When this is observed in casework caution should be exercised as this may indicate the presence of pyrolysis products. This should be done by investigating whether other n-alkylbenzenes also have an enhanced intensity, and by checking the presence of other pyrolysis indicators such as styrene (see paragraph 5.3).

The profiles of the C_2-, C_3-, and C_4-alkylbenzenes are illustrated in Figure 6.8 (top and middle). These profiles are not typical for gasoline, they are also observed in medium and heavy petroleum distillates (MPDs and HPDs). The difference lies in the intensity of the aromatics versus the alkanes. The same applies for the profiles of naphthalene and the methylnaphthalenes, illustrated in Figure 6.8 (bottom). Caution is necessary, if the naphthalene intensity is enhanced and/or if the ratio of the methylnaphthalenes is different from the one shown in Figure 6.8. These are usually indicators for pyrolysis.

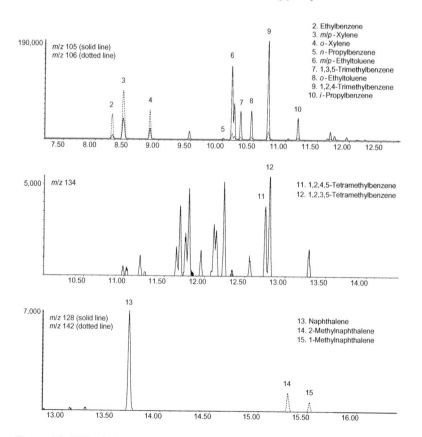

Figure 6.8 EIC m/z *105 + 106,* m/z *134, and* m/z *128 + 142 of a common gasoline composition (TD-GCMS).*

The indane profile at *m/z* 117 is illustrated in Figure 6.9. This figure shows that the indane profile of gasoline is different from that of HPDs. In (fresh) gasoline indane is generally more abundant than the methylindanes at *m/z* 117, while in petroleum distillates the methylindanes are generally more abundant than indane.

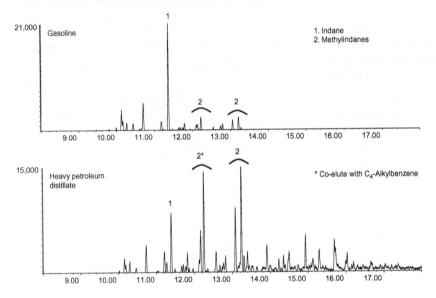

Figure 6.9 EIC m/z 117 of a gasoline and a HPD (TD-GCMS).

6.2.2.3 Oxygenates Composition

Oxygenates are employed as gasoline additives for different reasons:

- to reduce the carbon monoxide that is created during the burning of the fuel (to meet the clean air requirement);
- to raise the octane number of the fuel (as octane enhancer);
- to meet the Directive 2003/30/EC of the European Parliament and of the Council [33], that fuels should contain a certain percentage of biocomponents.

The oxygenates most commonly encountered in European gasolines are ethanol, MTBE, and/or ETBE. The composition of oxygenates may vary with each brand, and with each blend within a brand. An example of an oxygenate composition is illustrated in Figure 6.10. Note the small, broadened peak for ethanol, the result of the low affinity of Tenax® (the adsorbent used in the employed headspace sampling method) for this compound.

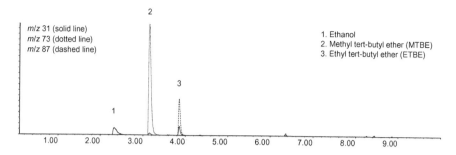

Figure 6.10 EIC m/z *31 + 73 + 87 of a random gasoline (TD-GCMS).*

Other oxygenates used in gasoline include isopropanol (IPA), *n*-butanol, TAME, and TAEE [34].

Due to their volatility and water-solubility, the oxygenates may not always be recovered in sufficient quantities from fire debris samples.

6.2.3 Presence of Particular Refinery Products

Gasoline is a blend product of different refinery process-streams. The blend composition may vary from refinery to refinery, and within a refinery from blend to blend[4]. As a result, the composition of gasoline may vary from blend to blend as discussed and illustrated in previous paragraphs.

Some blend refinery-streams are mainly produced as blend-product for gasoline. An example is the alkylate product from the alkylation refinery-process. Alkylate is one of several products added to gasoline as an octane enhancer. The composition of this alkylate product consists of mainly C_8-alkanes (see paragraph 6.2.2.1), including isooctane (2,2,4-tri-methylpentane). Particular C_7-alkanes (one of which is 2,3-methylpen-tane), and to a lesser extend particular C_{12}-alkanes (one of which is 2,2,4,6,6-pentamethylheptane), may be present as well. When identified in a fire debris sample, these alkanes support the presence of a refinery product, such as gasoline, alkylate gasoline, and aviation gasoline. [32]

Other blend refinery-streams may be by-products from production processes employed for other purposes/applications than blend-products for gasoline. One such example is a by-product of the ethylene produc-tion through the pyrolysis (steam cracking) of a liquid feedstock, such

---

[4] Depending amongst others on the refinery processes and refinery conditions employed, and the crude oil composition used.

as naphtha [35]. This by-product is called pyrolysis gasoline, often referred to as pygas. Pygas consists mainly of unsaturated compounds (olefins, di-olefins, and aromatics), usually in the C_5–C_{12} boiling range, such as cyclopentadiene (CPD), dicyclopentadiene (DCPD), benzene, toluene, xylenes, and/or styrene. Due to its high reactivity, it is hydrotreated before being blended into gasoline [36]. This results, for example, in tetrahydrodicyclopentadiene (4H-DCPD) from DCPD. When 4H-DCPD is identified in a fire debris sample, possibly in combination with DCPD and/or dihydrodicyclopentadiene (2H-DCPD)—usually when the hydrotreatment was incomplete—the presence of these compounds indicates a refinery product. If present, they can be used as an additional indicator in identifying gasoline. The characteristic mass spectral fragments of DCPD, 2H-DCPD, and 4H-DCPD are listed in Table 6.2. A gasoline containing these compounds is illustrated in Figure 6.11, and their mass spectra are illustrated in Figure 6.12.

Table 6.2 Mass Spectral Fragment Ions of DCPD, 2H-DCPD, and 4H-DCPD	
Compound	Fragment Ion(s) (*m/z*)
DCPD	66, 67, 132
2H-DCPD	66, 67, 134
4H-DCPD	66, 67, 95, 121, 136

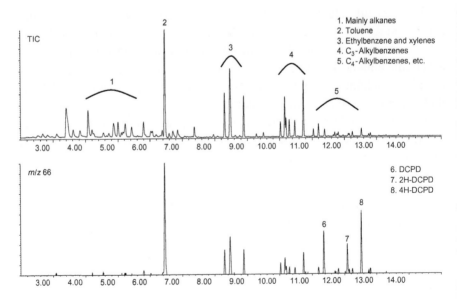

Figure 6.11 TIC and EIC m/z *66 of gasoline containing DCPD, 2H-DCPD, and 4H-DCPD (TD-GCMS).*

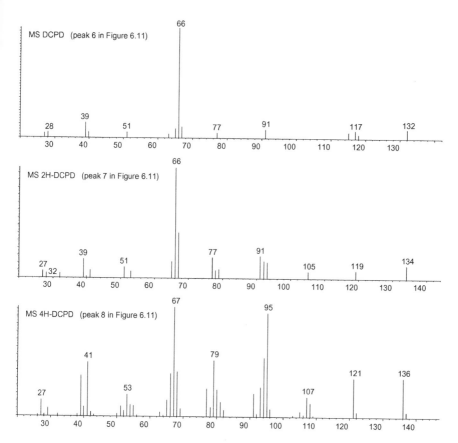

Figure 6.12 Mass spectra of DCPD, 2H-DCPD, and 4H-DCPD.

6.2.4 Effects that Alter the Composition of Gasoline

Partial evaporation, microbial degradation, and matrix/pyrolysis interference are phenomena that can be expected to occur in fire debris. The occurrence of these phenomena may alter the composition of the gasoline in the samples, resulting in distorted chromatograms. It may also interfere in the interpretation/judgement on whether gasoline is present or not.

6.2.4.1 Partial Evaporation

The changes in gasoline composition as a result of evaporation are illustrated in Figure 6.13. Caution is necessary when only the aromatic fraction is recovered from a fire debris sample. This aromatic fraction may originate either from residues of a heavily evaporated gasoline, or from an Aromatic Product. An example is discussed and illustrated in paragraph 6.2.5.

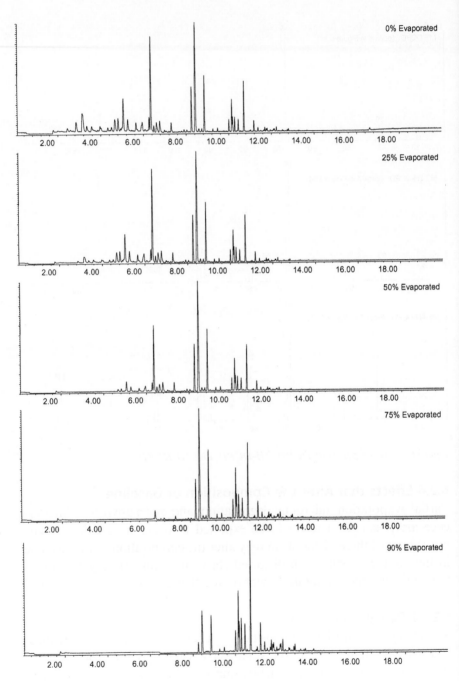

Figure 6.13 TICs of a gasoline at different degrees of evaporation (TD-GCMS).

6.2.4.2 Microbial Degradation

Residues of gasoline in fire debris samples with soil or vegetable material may show a certain degree of microbial degradation. The degree of microbial degradation depends heavily on the nature of the substrate material, storage-temperature, moisture-level, and time interval between sample collection and fire debris analysis [37–39]. The TICs of a gasoline at different degrees of degradation are illustrated in Figure 6.14a, some EICs in Figure 6.14b and c.

The susceptibility of the various components of gasoline to microbial degradation depends heavily on the type of bacteria present in the substrate. Some bacteria favor alkanes (n-alkanes will be primarily affected) whereas other bacteria favor aromatics (n-alkylbenzenes will be primarily affected).

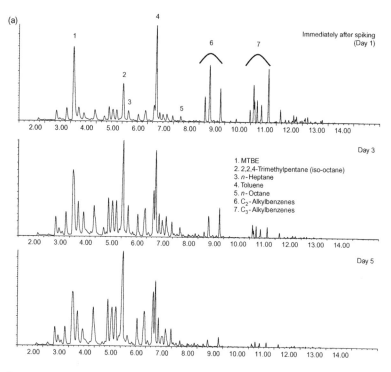

Figure 6.14 (a) TICs of a gasoline recovered from soil at different time intervals (TD-GCMS). (b) EIC m/z 71 of a gasoline recovered from soil at different time intervals (TD-GCMS). (c) EIC m/z 91 (solid line) and m/z 105 (dashed line) of a gasoline recovered from soil at different time intervals (TD-GCMS).

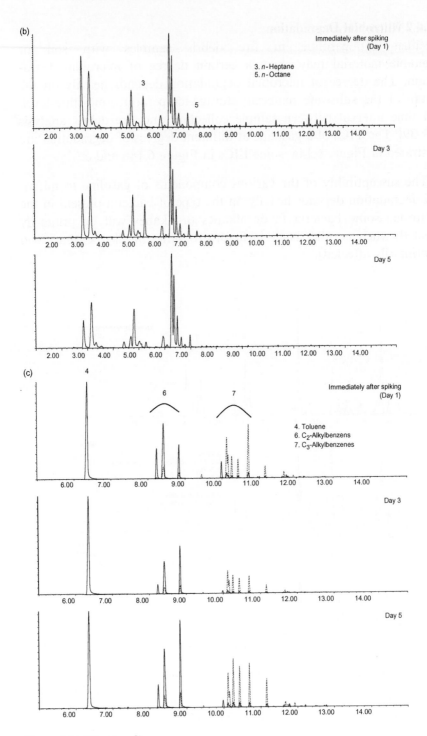

Figure 6.14 (Continued)

6.2.4.3 Matrix/Pyrolysis Interference

The identification of gasoline may be complicated by aromatic compounds that originate from combustion/pyrolysis of polymers, such as polyvinylchloride, polystyrene, and rubber products. Indicators of pyrolysis products are:

- An enhanced intensity of benzene, toluene, and higher *n*-alkylbenzenes (an example is illustrated in Figure 6.15).
- An enhanced intensity of isopropylbenzene (cumene).
- An enhanced intensity of naphthalene and different ratio of methylnaphthalenes.
- The presence of unsaturated compounds, such as styrene, α-methylstyrene, and 2,4-dimethylheptene.

In order to avoid a false positive identification of gasoline, caution is necessary when one or more of these indicators are observed. Additional indicators for the presence of burnt/pyrolyzed polymer materials are the lack of an alkane profile and oxygenates, which are typical for gasoline.

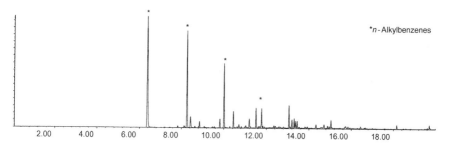

Figure 6.15 EIC m/z 91 of partially burnt/pyrolyzed carpet (TD-GCMS).

6.2.5 Composition of Gasoline Compared to Aromatic Products

Aromatic products consist almost exclusively of aromatic and/or condensed ring aromatic compounds. Alkanes are missing, or present only in insignificant amounts.

A heavily evaporated gasoline, in which the typical alkane fraction and oxygenates are no longer present, may not be distinguishable from an Aromatic Product. The TIC and EICs of an aromatic product (technical solvent in a commercial product sold as "roof primer") is illustrated in Figure 6.16, and compared to 75% and 90% evaporated gasoline in Figure 6.17.

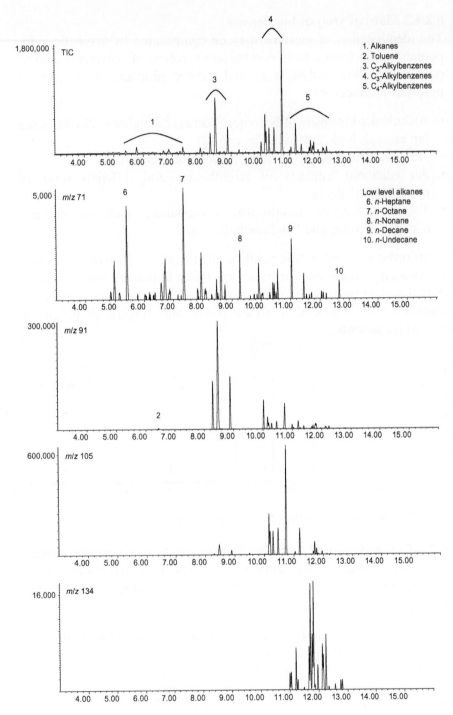

Figure 6.16 TIC and EICs of Aromatic Product (technical solvent in product sold as "roof primer"; TD-GCMS).

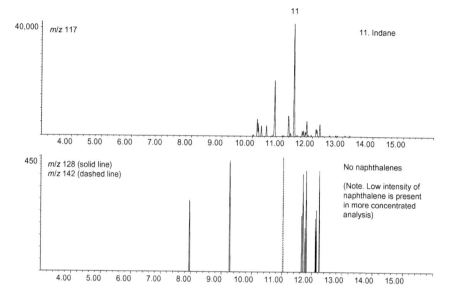

Figure 6.16 (Continued)

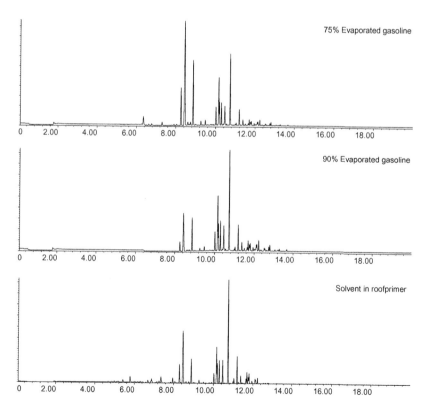

Figure 6.17 TIC of 75% evaporated gasoline, 90% evaporated gasoline, and technical solvent in roof primer (TD-GCMS).

6.2.6 Composition of Gasoline Compared to Alkylate Gasoline

Alkylate gasoline is a motor gasoline that consists mainly of the alkanes from the alkylate refinery process, namely the C_8-alkanes (including 2,2,4-trimethylpentane, also called isooctane) and to a lesser extend the C_7-alkanes (including 2,3-methylpentane) [32]. These alkanes are also present in conventional gasolines. Compared to conventional gasoline, the aromatic content in alkylate gasoline is low or nil. The oxygenates, which can be added to conventional gasoline, can be present as additives in alkylate gasoline as well. In the Netherlands the most commonly encountered oxygenate in alkylate gasoline is MTBE. Pure alkylate gasoline falls into the class "Isoparaffinic Products". Alkylate gasoline that contains aromatic hydrocarbons (at relative low concentration level) and/or oxygenate(s), falls into the class "Other-Miscellaneous".

Due to its low aromatic content, alkylate gasoline is often referred to as "cleaner burning gasoline" or "green gasoline". It is claimed that the fumes from alkylate gasoline are less toxic than those from conventional gasoline. For that reason alkylate gasoline is mainly used in hand carried machines such as chainsaws.

The composition of two alkylate gasolines (with and without oxygenates) compared to a conventional gasoline is illustrated in Figure 6.18.

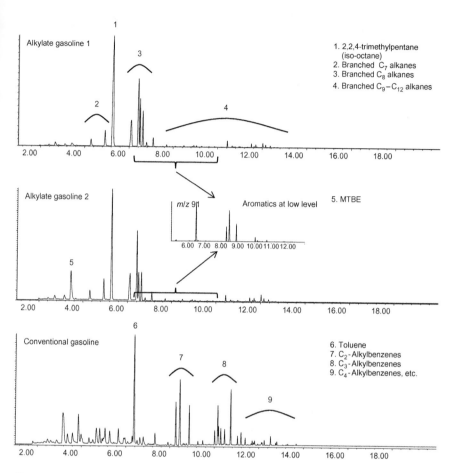

Figure 6.18 TICs of Alkylate gasolines compared to a conventional gasoline (TD-GCMS).

6.2.7 Summary of Characteristics for the Identification of Gasoline

Gasoline is characterized by the composition in Table 6.3, which should be demonstrated for a positive identification of gasoline in fire debris analysis results.

Table 6.3 Characteristics of Gasoline			
Compound Family	Presence	Characteristics	Paragraph Reference
Alkanes	Present	Normal-, branched-, and cycloalkanes predominantly in the range of C_6-C_9, in a composition that can be expected for gasoline	6.2.2.1; 6.2.3
Aromatics	Present	C_1-C_4-alkylbenzenes, indane and methylindanes, and often naphthalene and methylnaphthalenes, in a composition that can be expected for gasoline	6.2.2.2
Oxygenates	Can be present	Alcohols and/or ethers, which are specified in EN 228[a] (e.g., ethanol, IPA, n-butanol, MTBE, ETBE, TAEE, TAME), composition may vary	6.2.2.3
[a]European Standard EN 228:2012. Automotive fuels—unleaded petrol—requirements and test methods.			

The alkane fraction in gasoline can contain particular refinery-streams. The presence of these streams can support the identification of gasoline:

- Alkylate refinery-stream, characterized by: 2,2,4-trimethylpentane (isooctane), 2,3,4-trimethylpentane and other C_8-alkanes, and/or C_{12}-alkanes; see paragraphs 6.2.2.1 and 6.2.3.
- Pyrolysis gasoline (pygas) refinery-stream after hydrotreatment, characterized by: DCPD, 2H-DCPD, and/or 4H-DCPD; see paragraph 6.2.3.

If one or more gasoline characteristics are not met, further explanations for the identified components in the fire debris analysis results should be considered. For example:

- The absence of alkanes (including alkylate), oxygenates, and pygas indicators may indicate an Aromatic Product; see paragraph 6.2.5.
- The abundant presence of alkylate in combination with the absence or low presence of aromatics may indicate Alkylate gasoline of the class "Isoparaffinic Products"; see paragraph 6.2.6.
- The presence of alkenes, in combination with the absence of branched alkanes (including alkylate), oxygenates, and pygas indicators, may indicate pyrolysis products.

6.3 PETROLEUM DISTILLATES

6.3.1 Introduction

Petroleum distillates are crude oil refining fractions from the first refining process, the atmospheric distillation. These so-called "straight-run" or "conventional" distillates are characterized by dominating alkanes: mainly n-alkanes, and, at relatively lower concentration levels, branched alkanes and cycloalkanes in a typical crude oil "fingerprint" pattern. Originally, they also contain a relatively low content of aromatics (boiling range dependent), if the distillate fraction is not de-aromatized. Although the de-aromatized fractions are further refined, in ASTM E1618 they are classified under the same class as the conventional petroleum distillates.

In ASTM E1618, the petroleum distillates are divided into three subclasses based on boiling (n-alkane) range: light, medium, and heavy.

The number of petroleum distillate products, or commercial/industrial products containing a petroleum distillate as an ingredient, is huge. Product examples can be found in Tables 5.1 and 6.4 of this guideline, and in Table 1 of ASTM E1618:14 [1]. Within each subclass, the boiling range of these distillates may vary (slightly). The overall composition of each subclass is discussed and illustrated in the following paragraphs.

Table 6.4 Petroleum Distillate Subclasses			
Subclass	Product Examples	Approximate Boiling Range (°C)	Carbon Atoms Range
LPD	Cleaning spirit, dry cleaning naphtha, benzine, lighter fluid, petroleum ether, coleman fuel, paint thinner	0–150	C_4–C_9
MPD	White spirit, mineral spirits, brush cleaner, petroleum, paint thinner, metal degreaser	125–225	C_8–C_{13}
HPD	Kerosene, petroleum, lamp oil, torch oil, brush cleaner, barbecue lighter fluid, jet fuel, gasoil, diesel fuel, heating oil	150–350	C_9–C_{20+}

The boiling ranges of some distillates do not fit neatly into one of the above subclasses. According to ASTM E1618, these products should then be classified as "light to medium", or "medium to heavy". An example of such a distillate is illustrated in paragraph 6.3.5.

Some commercial or industrial products contain a petroleum distillate fraction which is blended with other components, such as alcohols and ethers, or with products from other classes, such as Aromatic Products. These blend products are often sold for specific applications. Examples of such blend products are illustrated in paragraph 6.3.8.

6.3.2 Light Petroleum Distillates

6.3.2.1 Introduction

LPDs consist of alkanes (normal-, branched-, and cycloalkanes) in the range of C_4–C_9. Aromatics are normally absent, or present only as insignificant amounts. Fragment ions of the alkane family in LPDs are listed in Table 6.5.

Table 6.5 Fragment ions for LPD		
Compound Family	**(Group of) Compound(s)**	**Fragment Ion(s) (*m/z*)**
Alkanes	*n*-Alkanes, branched alkanes	43, 57, 71, 85, ...
	Cycloalkanes	41, 55, 69, 83, 97, ...[a]

[a]Note that cycloalkanes and alkenes share the same fragment ions, but can be differentiated based on retention time and mass spectra.

6.3.2.2 Overall Composition of LPD

The TIC of a LPD shows alkanes (normal-, branched-, and cycloalkanes), predominately in the range of C_4–C_9. The boiling range of LPDs may vary, and depends on the refinery distillation conditions[5] employed. Within the boiling range, the composition should resemble that of the crude oil(s) used. TIC examples of LPDs are illustrated in Figure 6.19.

[5] Determined by the specifications of the end product.

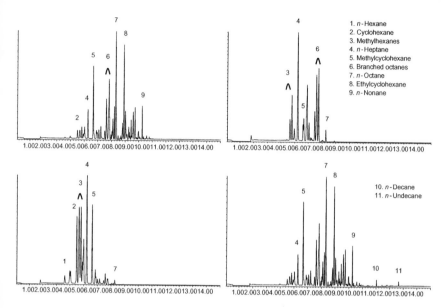

Figure 6.19 TICs of different LPDs (TD-GCMS).

An example of fragment ions of a wide-range LPD is illustrated in Figure 6.20. Such a composition is sold as "cleaning spirit" and "dry cleaning naphtha". When considering the presence of LPD in fire debris, the presence of this compound family, including the patterns and relative concentrations levels within and between its fragment ions, should be reviewed. Fragment ions of other components (such as aromatics and oxygenates) are not illustrated because they are absent in a conventional LPD. However, in the evaluation process of fire debris analysis results, they should be reviewed.

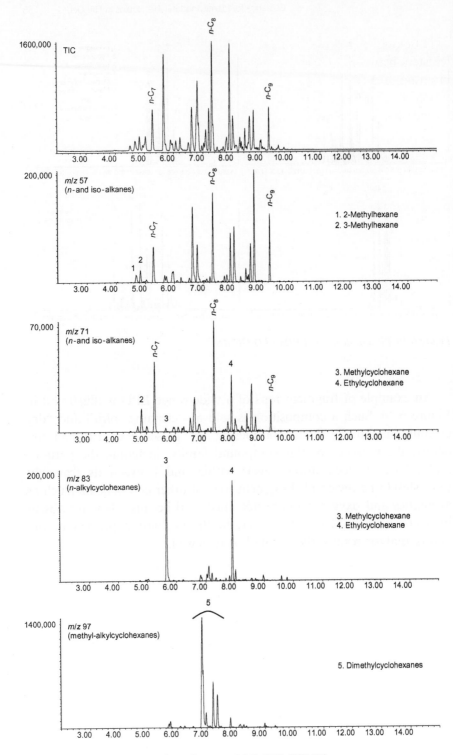

Figure 6.20 TIC and EICs of a wide-range LPD (TD-GCMS).

Looking at fragment ion 71, the alkane pattern shows triplet-like clusters between n-C$_6$ and n-C$_9$; these are considered characteristic for a straight-run LPD[6]. These clusters originate from crude oil, as illustrated in Figure 6.21. They are also seen in the naphtha fraction from crude oil, the refinery fraction of LPD, see Figure 6.22.

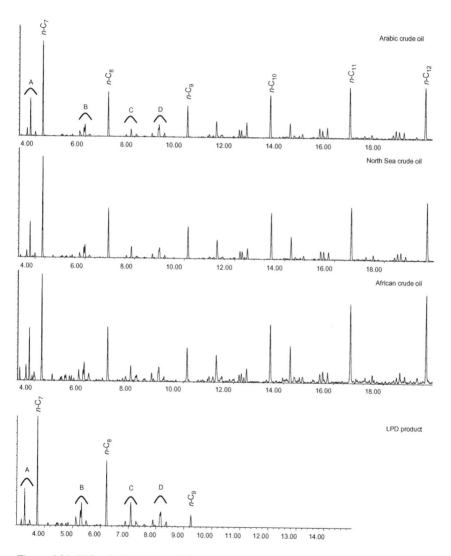

Figure 6.21 EIC m/z 71 of three different crude oils versus a conventional LPD (GCMS of pentane dilution).

---

[6] Note that the observed alkane pattern may depend on the GC-conditions employed.

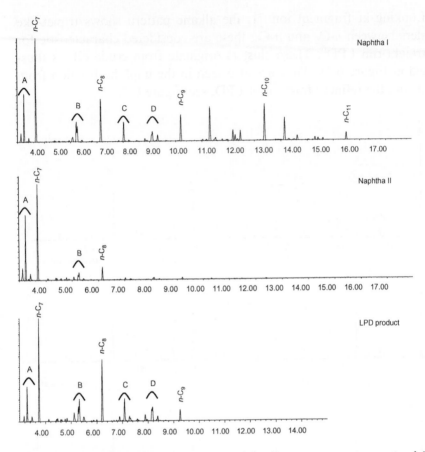

Figure 6.22 EIC m/z 71 of two different naphtha fractions versus a conventional LPD (GCMS of pentane dilution).

Fragment ion 83 shows the *n*-alkyl cyclohexanes as the most abundant compounds. They are also considered typical for crude oil. The most abundant *n*-alkyl cyclohexanes in any LPD are usually methyl- and/or ethyl cyclohexane, depending on the boiling range of the LPD product. Fragment ion 97 may also show methyl-alkylcyclohexanes, their presence again depending on the boiling range of the LPD product.

The alkane pattern of fragment ion 71 of LPD is quite distinctive from alkane fractions/products which are either more refined or obtained from other refinery processes. One example is the alkane fraction in most gasolines as shown in Figure 6.23. In gasoline with little or no naphtha fraction, the cluster marked A showing branched C_7-alkanes may be present, but with a higher intensity than the intensity level of *n*-C_7-alkane compared to that in crude oil. In these gasolines the clusters B–D are not visible.

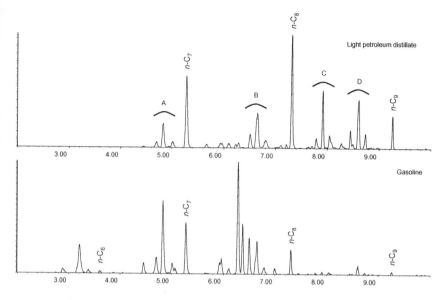

Figure 6.23 EIC m/z 71 of a LPD and gasoline (TD-GCMS).

For other examples of alkane fractions, see some technical solvents in paragraph 6.9 (class "Other-Miscellaneous").

6.3.2.3 Effects that Alter the Composition of LPD

Important effects that may influence the composition of LPD residues in fire debris samples are evaporation and microbial degradation.

6.3.2.3.1 Partial Evaporation

LPD residues in fire debris samples may show some degree of evaporation, due to the volatile nature of these products. Different degrees of evaporation of a wide-range LPD are illustrated in Figure 6.24.

6.3.2.3.2 Microbial Degradation

LPD residues in fire debris samples that contain soil or vegetable material may show microbial degradation. As mentioned in paragraph 6.2.4, the degree of microbial degradation depends heavily on the type of microorganisms present, the nature of the substrate material, storage-temperature, moisture-level, and time interval between sample collection and fire debris analysis. In general, n-alkanes are more sensitive to degradation than branched alkanes, and cycloalkanes are the least affected by microbial attack [37–39].

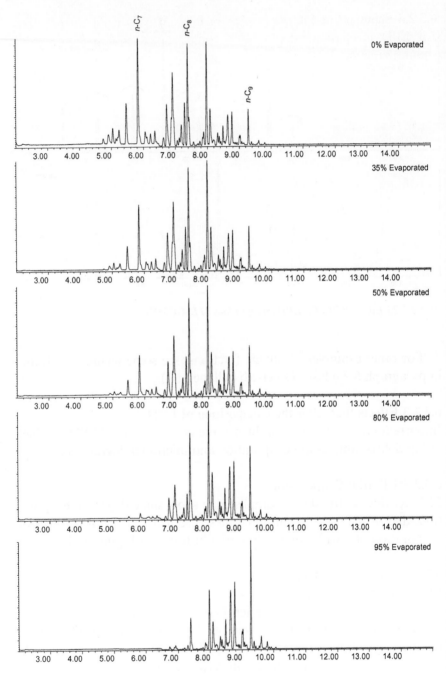

Figure 6.24 TICs of a wide-range LPD at different degrees of evaporation (TD-GCMS).

6.3.2.4 Summary of Characteristics for the Identification of LPD

An LPD is characterized by the composition in Table 6.6, which should be demonstrated for a positive identification of an LPD in fire debris analysis results.

Table 6.6 Characteristics of a LPD			
Compound Family	Presence	Characteristics	Paragraph Reference
Alkanes	Present	Normal-, branched-, and cycloalkanes predominantly in the range of C_4-C_9. Branched- and cycloalkanes in a characteristic crude oil fingerprint pattern at m/z 71 (i.e., typical triplet-like clusters)	6.3.2.2
Aromatics	Absent, or present in insignificant amounts	Alkylbenzenes in the corresponding carbon range	
Oxygenates	Absent		

If the LPD characteristics are not met, further explanations for the presence of the identified components in the fire debris analysis results should be considered. For example:

- The absence (or reduced presence) of n-alkanes may indicate microbial degradation or a Naphthenic-Paraffinic Product; see paragraphs 6.3.2.3 and 6.6.
- The absence of n-alkanes and cycloalkanes may indicate an Isoparaffinic Product; see paragraph 6.4.
- The absence of an alkane pattern that is characteristic for crude oil (triplet-like clusters) at m/z 71, perhaps in combination with the abundant presence of other type of components, may indicate a technical solvent of class "Oxygenated Solvents" or "Other-Miscellaneous"; see paragraphs 6.8 and 6.9.

6.3.3 Medium Petroleum Distillates

6.3.3.1 Introduction

Straight-run MPDs consist of alkanes (normal-, branched-, and cycloalkanes), and aromatics, predominantly in the range of C_8-C_{13}. The n-alkanes are dominant and their pattern is associated with a

Gaussian-like distribution. Aromatics are also present in MPDs, but are less abundant than the alkanes.

For specific applications, the aromatics may be significantly reduced or completely removed by further refinement (de-aromatization) of the distillates. These fractions are classified as (de-aromatized) MPDs as well.

Fragment ions for MPDs are listed in Table 6.7.

Table 6.7 Fragment Ions for MPDs		
Compound Family	(Group of) Compound(s)	Fragment Ion(s) (m/z)
Alkanes	n-Alkanes, branched alkanes	43, 57, 71, 85, ...
	Cycloalkanes	41, 55, 69, 83, 97, ...[a]
Aromatics	Toluene	91
	C_2-Alkylbenzenes	91, 106
	C_3-Alkylbenzenes	91, 105, 120
	C_4-Alkylbenzenes	91, 119, 134
	Indane	117
	Methylindanes	117, 132
	Naphthalene	128
	Methylnaphthalenes	142

[a]Note that cycloalkanes and alkenes share the same fragment ions, but can be differentiated based on retention time and mass spectra.

6.3.3.2 Overall Composition of MPD

The TIC of a MPD shows alkanes (normal-, branched-, and cycloalkanes), predominantly in the range of C_8-C_{13}, as most abundant components. The boiling range of MPDs may vary, and depends on the refinery distillation conditions[7] employed. Within the relevant boiling range, the composition should resemble that of the crude oil(s) used, unless the product is de-aromatized. TIC examples of MPDs are illustrated in Figure 6.25.

---

[7] Determined by the specifications of the end product.

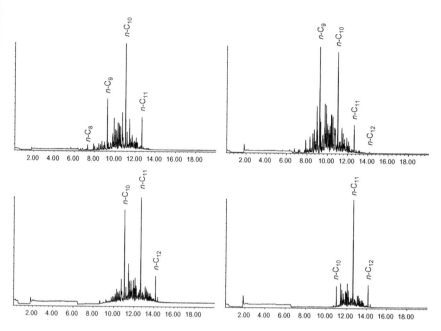

Figure 6.25 TICs of different MPDs (TD-GCMS).

An example of fragment ions of the different compound families in a conventional MPD is illustrated in Figure 6.26. This composition is found in products which are sold as "mineral spirit" and "white spirit". When considering the presence of an MPD in fire debris, the presence/absence of these compound families should be reviewed, including their patterns and relative concentrations levels (within and between compound families).

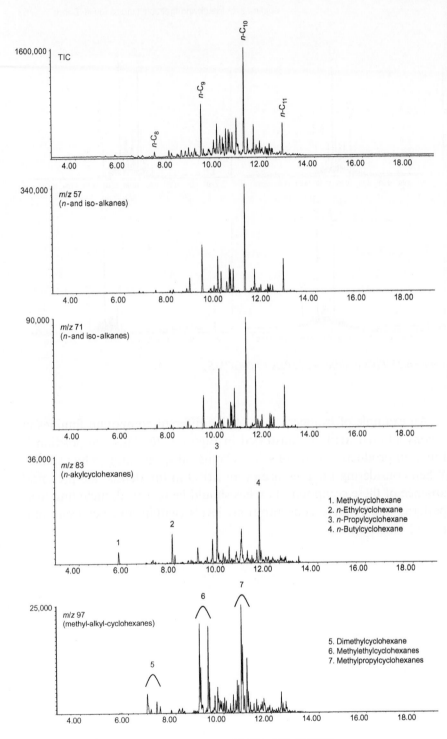

Figure 6.26 TIC and EICs of a conventional MPD (TD-GCMS).

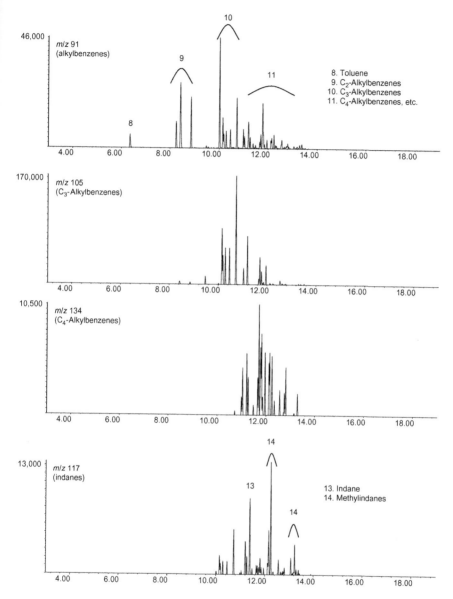

Figure 6.26 (Continued)

Fragment ions 57 and 71 show the most abundant components (the alkanes) of an MPD. The *n*-alkanes are dominant, and represent a Gaussian-like distribution as a result of the distillation process. The branched alkanes and cycloalkanes show a fingerprint pattern that is characteristic for crude oil. Due to variations in the composition of crude oils from different sources, small variations in the fingerprint pattern can be expected between distillates. A comparison between a wide-range conventional MPD and a crude oil fingerprint pattern is illustrated in Figure 6.27.

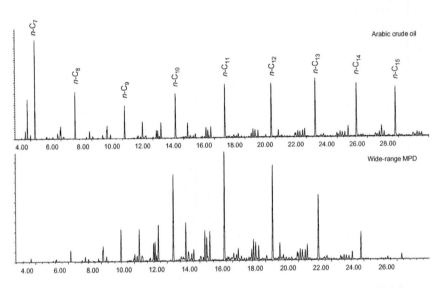

Figure 6.27 EIC m/z 71 of Arabic crude oil and a wide-range MPD (GCMS of pentane dilution).

Fragment ions 83 and 97 in Figure 6.26 show the alkylcyclohexanes, which are considered typical for crude oil, as the most abundant compounds. Amongst the alkylcyclohexanes, the *n*-alkylcyclohexanes are the most abundant, but their intensities are relatively low compared to the intensity levels of the *n*-alkanes[8]. The *n*-alkylcyclohexanes generally represent a Gaussian-like distribution, if the boiling range of the MPD is wide enough and contains more than two consecutive *n*-alkylcyclohexanes.

---

[8] Note that in MPDs, the relative intensity level of alkylcyclohexanes compared to *n*-alkanes is considerably lower than in LPDs.

In straight-run MPDs fragment ions 91, 105, and 134 show the alkylbenzenes as the most abundant compounds. In de-aromatized MPDs they are absent or heavily reduced in intensity. Since the carbon range of MPDs ranges approximately from C_8 to C_{13}, toluene is absent, or present at low intensity level. The patterns of the aromatics resemble those of the crude oil(s) used.

Fragment ion 117 shows the indanes of crude oil as the most abundant components. Note that in Figure 6.26, the peaks representing the first cluster of methylindanes co-elute with C_4-alkylbenzenes (which contain low levels of ion 117). The degree of co-elution depends on the GC-conditions employed (e.g., column, temperature program).

Naphthalenes may be present in MPDs as well. Their presence depends on the boiling range of the distillate.

6.3.3.3 Composition of Conventional MPD Compared to De-Aromatized MPD

De-aromatized MPDs are straight-run products which are further refined to remove or reduce the level of aromatics. The alkane composition of de-aromatized MPDs should resemble that of crude oil. The TIC and EIC 71 and 83 of a de-aromatized MPD (sold as "odorless white spirit") compared to a conventional MPD (sold as "white spirit") are illustrated in Figure 6.28a–c.

6.3.3.4 Composition of Conventional MPD Compared to Dewaxed MPD

Dewaxing is a process that is used to remove (a certain degree of) wax[9] from a petroleum distillate fraction, in order to meet the low temperature properties[10] required[11] for its application [40]. An example is the (partial) dewaxing of HPD diesel fuel for cold areas, to avoid wax compounds separating out and causing engine problems [40].

A common process is catalytic dewaxing, which involves selective hydroisomerization and hydrocracking of normal and slightly

---

[9] Mainly *n*-alkanes.

[10] The required values for cloud point, pour point, and cold filter plugging point.

[11] To avoid crystallization at low temperature.

branched alkanes. As a result, the end product has no, or a reduced level of *n*-alkanes, and a branched alkane fingerprint pattern that may no longer resemble that of crude oil. Cycloalkanes are still present.

An example of an MPD that looks partially dewaxed *and* de-aromatized, is illustrated in Figure 6.28a–c. This product is sold as "odourless white spirit". The composition of this product no longer shows the characteristics for classification as a de-aromatized MPD: *n*-alkanes are present but not dominating, and the branched alkane fingerprint pattern at *m/z* 71 differs from what is expected for crude oil. Classification as a technical product from the class "Naphthenic-Paraffinic Product" should be considered instead.

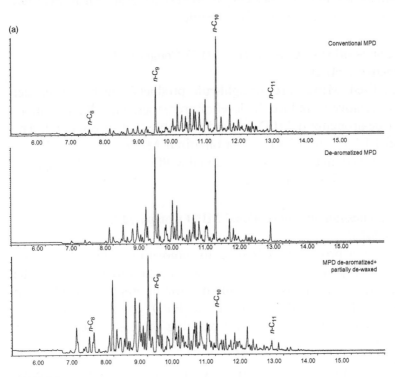

Figure 6.28 (a) TIC of conventional MPD, de-aromatized MPD, and MPD de-aromatized + partially dewaxed (TD-GCMS). (b) EIC m/z 71 of conventional MPD, de-aromatized MPD, and MPD de-aromatized + partially dewaxed (TD-GCMS). (c) EIC m/z 83 of conventional MPD, de-aromatized MPD, and MPD de-aromatized + partially dewaxed (TD-GCMS).

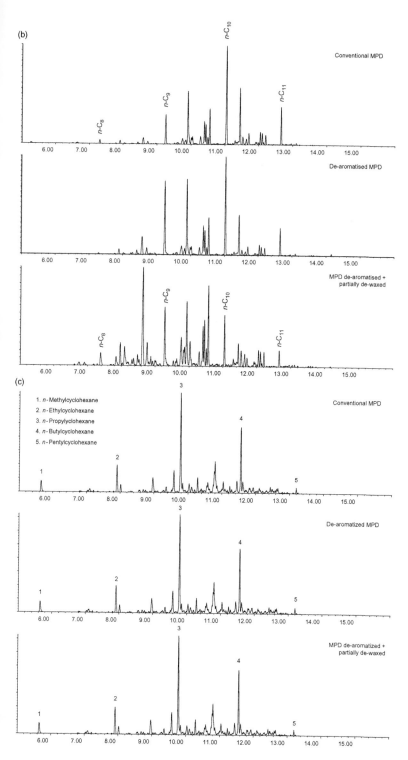

Figure 6.28 (Continued)

6.3.3.5 Effects that Alter the Composition of MPD

Evaporation and microbial degradation are important effects that may alter the composition of MPD residues in fire debris samples.

6.3.3.5.1 Partial Evaporation

Different degrees of evaporation of an MPD are illustrated in Figure 6.29.

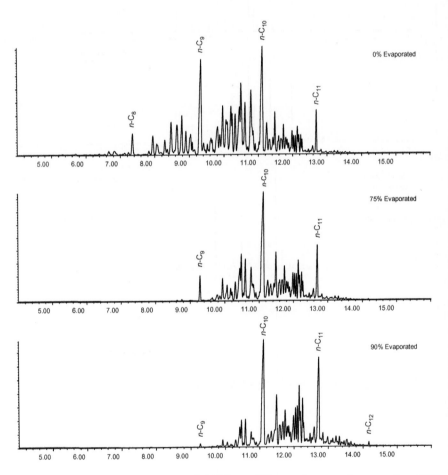

Figure 6.29 TICs of a conventional MPD at different degrees of evaporation (TD-GCMS).

6.3.3.5.2 Microbial Degradation

MPD residues in fire debris samples that contain soil or vegetable material may show a certain degree of microbial degradation. As mentioned in paragraphs 6.2.4 and 6.3.2.3, the degree of microbial degradation depends heavily on the type of microorganisms present, the nature of the material, storage-temperature, moisture-level, and time interval between sample collection and fire debris analysis. In general, n-alkanes are more sensitive to degradation than branched alkanes, and cycloalkanes are the least affected [37–39]. A partially degraded straight-run MPD, showing a reduced intensity level of n-alkanes, may be difficult to distinguish from a partially dewaxed MPD. Indications for degradation rather than dewaxing may be found in the composition of the aromatics and perhaps in the composition of the branched alkanes.

6.3.3.6 Summary of Characteristics for the Identification of MPD

A MPD is characterized by the composition in Table 6.8, which should be demonstrated for a positive identification of a MPD in fire debris analysis results.

Table 6.8 Characteristics of a MPD			
Compound Family	Presence	Characteristics	Paragraph Reference
Alkanes	Present	A Gaussian-like distribution of normal-, branched-, and cycloalkanes, predominantly in the range of C_8–C_{13}. n-Alkanes are prominent, branched alkanes and cycloalkanes in a characteristic crude oil fingerprint pattern at m/z 71, and cycloalkane(s) are dominant at m/z 83	6.3.3.2
Aromatics	Present in straight-run MPD, absent or present in insignificant amounts in de-aromatized MPD	Alkylbenzenes, indane and methylindanes, and possibly naphthalene and methylnaphthalenes in the corresponding carbon range	6.3.3.2
Oxygenates	Absent		

If one or more of the MPD characteristics are not met, further explanations for the presence of the identified components in the fire debris analysis results should be considered. For example:

- The absence (or reduced presence) of n-alkanes may indicate microbial degradation; see paragraph 6.3.3.5.
- The absence of n-alkanes (or reduced presence) and aromatics may indicate a Naphthenic-Paraffinic Product; see paragraph 6.6.
- The absence of n-alkanes, cycloalkanes, and aromatics may indicate an Isoparaffinic Product; see paragraph 6.4.
- The absence of a characteristic crude oil (fingerprint) pattern (including cycloalkanes) and aromatics may indicate a Normal Alkane-Isoparaffinic Product of class "Other-Miscellaneous"; see paragraph 6.9.
- The abundant presence of other types of components may indicate a technical solvent of class "Oxygenated Solvents" or "Other-Miscellaneous"; see paragraphs 6.8 and 6.9.

6.3.4 Heavy Petroleum Distillates
6.3.4.1 Introduction
Straight-run HPDs consist of alkanes (normal-, branched-, and cycloalkanes), and aromatics, predominantly in the range of C_9-C_{20+}. The n-alkanes are dominant and their pattern is associated with a Gaussian-like distribution[12]. spanning at least five consecutive n-alkanes (note: there may be less than 5, in case of narrow-range product starting above n-C_{11}). Aromatics are present, but are less abundant than the alkanes.

For specific applications, the aromatics may be significantly reduced or completely removed by further refinement (de-aromatization) of the distillates. These fractions are classified as (de-aromatized) HPDs as well.

Compound families with corresponding mass spectral fragments of HPDs are listed in Table 6.9.

---

[12] Exceptions can be diesel oil and heating oils, which are often blends of different refinery fractions (from primary and secondary distillation). As a result, the consecutive series of n-alkanes is dominantly present but does not represent a Gaussian-like distribution, as can be seen in Figure 6.30.

Table 6.9 Fragment Ions for HPDs

Compound Family	(Group of) Compound(s)	Fragment Ion(s) (*m/z*)
Alkanes	*n*-Alkanes, branched alkanes	43, 57, 71, 85, ...
	Cycloalkanes	41, 55, 69, 83, 97, ...[a]
Aromatics	Toluene	91
	C_2-Alkylbenzenes	91, 106
	C_3-Alkylbenzenes	91, 105, 120
	C_4-Alkylbenzenes	91, 119, 134
	Indane	117
	Methylindanes	117, 132
	Naphthalene	128
	Methylnaphthalenes	142

[a]Note that cycloalkanes and alkenes share the same fragment ions, but can be differentiated based on retention time and mass spectra.

A percentage of fatty acid esters may be blended into HPD products designed for a specific application (i.e., fuel for diesel engines). This so-called biodiesel blend, usually consists mainly of $C_{16}-C_{18}$ FAMEs. The fatty acids of these FAMEs originate from vegetable oil. Fatty acid esters are added to HPD diesel oil to meet the European Union decision on fuels [41]. The percentage of biodiesel in petroleum diesel may vary from blend to blend, as illustrated in Figure 6.31. Fragment ions of these FAMEs are 74 and 87 (saturated FAMEs), 55 (single unsaturated FAMEs), and 67 (double unsaturated FAMEs).

6.3.4.2 Overall Composition of HPD

The TIC of a HPD shows alkanes (normal-, branched-, and cycloalkanes), predominantly in the range of C_9-C_{20+}, as the most abundant components. The boiling range of HPDs may vary, and depends on the refinery distillation conditions[13] employed. It may (partially) overlap with the boiling range of an LPD and/or MPD. Within the relevant boiling range, the composition should resemble that of the crude oil(s) used, unless the product is de-aromatized.

---

[13] Determined by the specifications of the end product.

In fire debris analysis, it will depend on the method and conditions employed, to what extent the least volatile part of a wide-range HPD (i.e., C_9-C_{20+}), such as diesel oil and heating oil (i.e., gasoil) will be recovered. To illustrate the effect of the recovery and analysis method, an example of a diesel fuel, analyzed by liquid injection and via preconcentrated heated (70 °C) headspace analysis is illustrated in Figure 6.30. Note that the difference in retention times between both chromatograms is the result of the fact that both analyses are performed on different instruments with different GC temperature conditions.

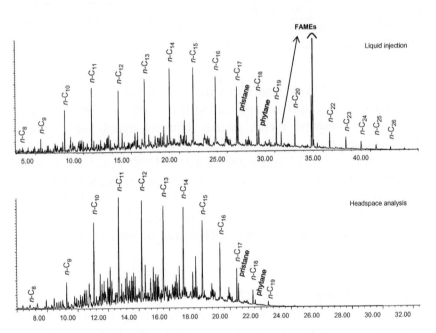

Figure 6.30 TICs of HPD diesel oil, liquid injection (GCMS of pentane dilution), and headspace analysis (TD-GCMS).

A full-range HPD (gasoil) may show a similar chromatogram to that of an HPD with a smaller boiling range (kerosene products) as a consequence of headspace analysis (and the conditions and type of the headspace method employed).

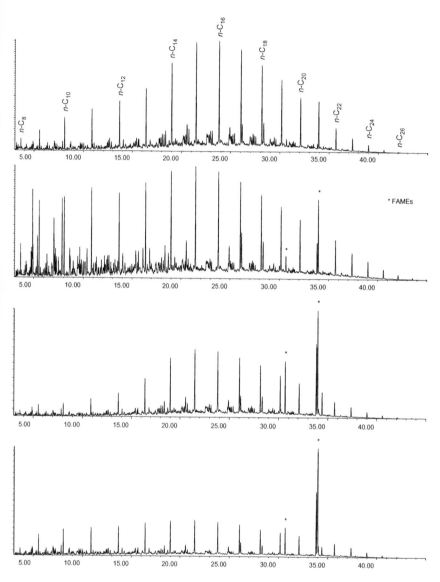

Figure 6.31 TICs of different HPD diesel oils with increasing level of biodiesel (from top to bottom; GCMS of pentane dilutions).

TIC examples of HPDs with different boiling ranges are illustrated in Figure 6.32. These TICs are obtained via liquid injections from pentane dilutions of the HPDs, to show the full boiling range of these products. In this way the discrimination effect between the least and most volatile components, which may occur with headspace analysis, is eliminated.

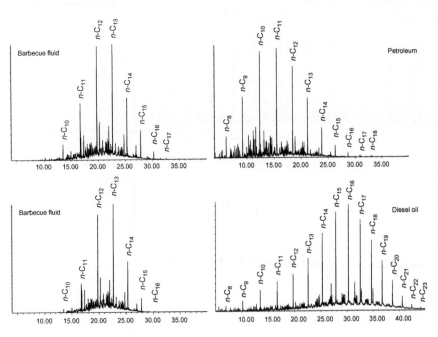

Figure 6.32 TICs of different HPDs obtained via liquid injection (GCMS of pentane dilution).

An example of fragment ions of the different compound families in a wide-range HPD is illustrated in Figure 6.33. This product is sold as "diesel fuel". When considering the presence of an HPD in fire debris, the presence/absence of these compound families should be reviewed, including their patterns and relative concentration levels (within and between compound families).

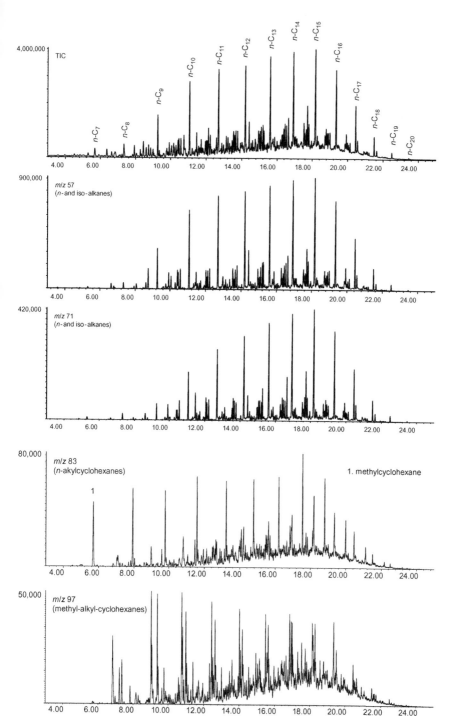

Figure 6.33 TIC and EICs of a wide-range HPD, a diesel oil (TD-GCMS).

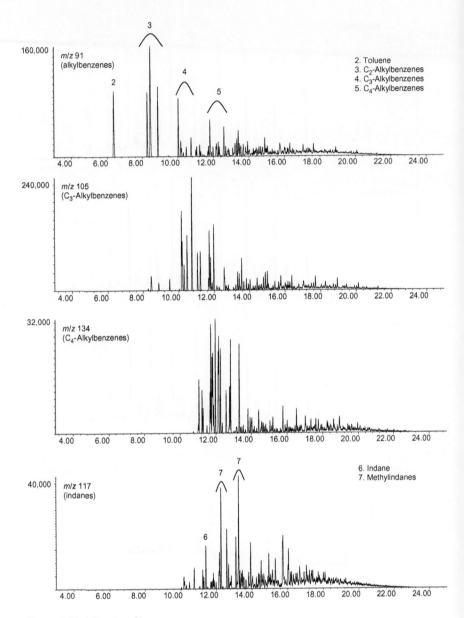

Figure 6.33 (Continued)

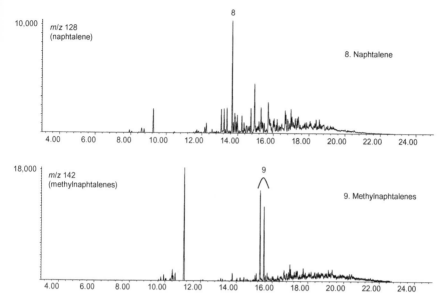

Figure 6.33 (Continued)

Fragment ions 57 and 71 show the most abundant components (the alkanes) of an HPD. The *n*-alkanes are dominant. In a straight-run HPD, they represent a Gaussian-like distribution[12] as a result of the distillation process. The branched alkanes and cycloalkanes show a fingerprint pattern that is characteristic for crude oil, including the isoprenoïds (crude oil biomarkers [42]) such as pristane and phytane. Between distillates from different crude oils, small variations in the fingerprint pattern can be expected due to variation in the composition of crude oils from different sources. An example of an HPD (diesel oil) compared to a crude oil pattern at fragment ion 71 is illustrated in Figure 6.34. A blow-up of the fingerprint pattern from both is illustrated in Figure 6.35.

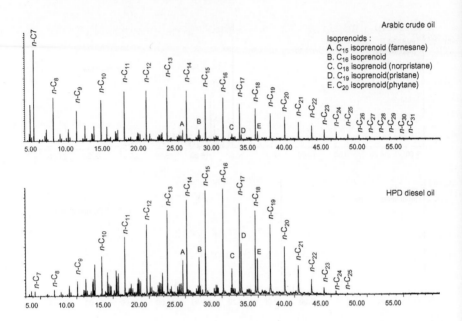

Figure 6.34 EIC m/z *71 of Arabic crude oil and HPD diesel oil (GCMS of pentane dilution).*

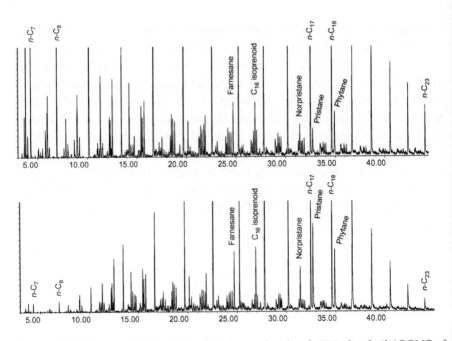

Figure 6.35 Blow-up of EIC m/z *71 of Arabic crude oil and HPD diesel oil (GCMS of pentane dilution).*

Fragment ions 83 and 97 in Figure 6.33 show the alkylcyclohexanes, which are considered typical for crude oil, as the most abundant compounds. Amongst the alkylcyclohexanes, the *n*-alkylcyclohexanes are the most abundant, but their intensities are relatively low compared to the intensity level of the *n*-alkanes[14]. The *n*-alkylcyclohexanes generally represent a Gaussian-like distribution, if the boiling range of the HPD is wide enough and contains more than two consecutive *n*-alkylcyclohexanes.

In straight-run HPDs fragment ions 91, 105, and 134 show the alkylbenzenes as the most abundant compounds. In de-aromatized HPDs they are absent or heavily reduced in intensity. Depending on the boiling range of a particular HPD, the most volatile aromatics (such as toluene) may be absent, or present at low intensity levels. The pattern of the aromatics resembles that of the crude oil(s) used.

Fragment ion 117 shows the indanes of crude oil as the most abundant components, with indane and the methylindanes being the most prominent. Ethylindanes and other compounds, such as methyltetrahydronaphthalenes, may be present at relatively lower intensity levels.

Note that in Figure 6.33, the peaks representing the first cluster of methylindanes co-elute with C_4-alkylbenzenes (which contain low levels of ion 117). The degree of co-elution depends on the GC-conditions employed (e.g., column, temperature program).

6.3.4.3 Composition of Conventional HPD Compared to De-Aromatized HPD

De-aromatized HPDs are straight-run products which are further refined to remove or reduce the level of aromatics. The alkane composition of de-aromatized HPDs should resemble that of crude oil. De-aromatized HPDs are, for example, sold as "petroleum" and as "petroleum for kerosene heaters without smoke discharger".

6.3.4.4 Composition of Conventional HPD Compared to Dewaxed HPD

See paragraph 6.3.3.4. No examples of a (partial) dewaxed HPD are available in the authors' reference collections to include as an illustration.

---

[14] Note that in HPDs, as in MPDs, the relative intensity level of alkylcyclohexanes compared to *n*-alkanes is considerably lower than in LPDs.

6.3.4.5 Composition of Conventional HPD Diesel Oil Compared to GTL Diesel Oil

GTL stands for gas-to-liquid (see paragraph 3.3.1). GTL diesel is a liquid fuel, obtained synthetically from natural gas[15], via the so-called Fischer-Tropsch process.

GTL diesel differs in composition from conventional petroleum diesel oil. As it is not a petroleum distillate, but obtained via the conversion of natural gas into "new" hydrocarbons, it does not contain the characteristics of crude oil as conventional petroleum diesel oils do. GTL diesels consist mainly of n-alkanes and a relatively small amount of branched alkanes. Isoprenoïds, cycloalkanes, and aromatics are absent. The composition of the branched alkanes is different from that of conventional petroleum diesel oils. Instead, it is similar to that of Isoparaffinic Products. The composition of GTL diesel resembles that of a Normal Alkane-Isoparaffinic Product. According to ASTM E1618 it should be classified as "Other-Miscellaneous", as "Normal Alkane-Isoparaffinic Products" is not a class defined by this standard.

GTL-diesel is considered to be an environmentally friendly fuel, due to the absence of aromatics. An example of a GTL-diesel compared to a conventional petroleum diesel oil is illustrated in Figure 6.36a−c.

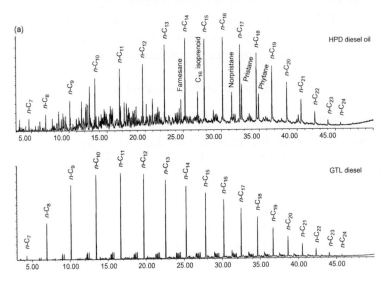

Figure 6.36 (a) TIC of a conventional diesel oil compared to a GTL diesel (GCMS of pentane dilution). (b) EIC m/z 71 of a conventional diesel oil compared to a GTL diesel (GCMS of pentane dilution). (c) EIC m/z 83 of a conventional diesel oil compared to a GTL diesel (GCMS of pentane dilution).

---

[15] Also called refinery gas, a boiling range fraction from crude oil, and therefore by itself a fossil fuel.

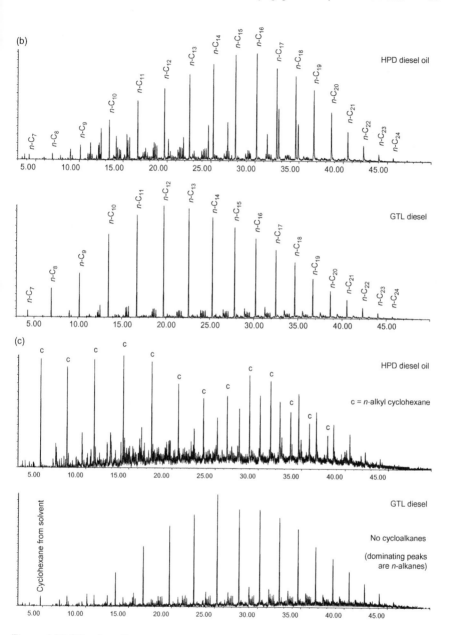

Figure 6.36 (Continued)

6.3.4.6 Effects that Alter the Composition of HPD

Important effects that may alter the composition of HPD residues in fire debris samples are evaporation, microbial degradation, and matrix interference.

6.3.4.6.1 Partial Evaporation

Different degrees of evaporation of an HPD diesel oil are illustrated in Figure 6.37.

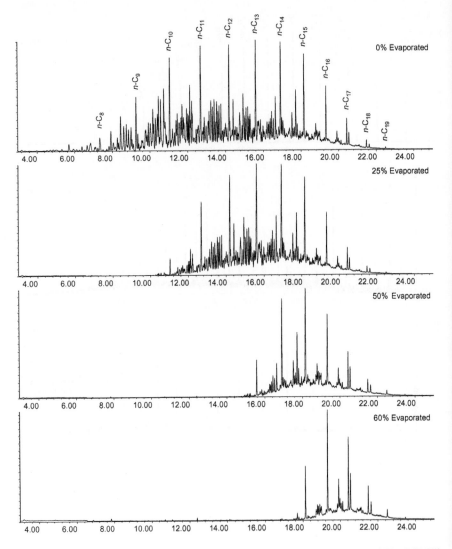

Figure 6.37 TICs of an HPD diesel oil at different degrees of evaporation (TD-GCMS).

6.3.4.6.2 Microbial Degradation

HPD residues in fire debris samples containing soil or vegetable material may show a certain degree of microbial degradation. As mentioned before, the degree of microbial degradation depends heavily on the type of microorganisms present, the nature of the substrate material, storage-temperature, moisture-level, and time interval between sample collection and fire debris analysis. In general, *n*-alkanes are more sensitive to degradation than branched alkanes, and cycloalkanes are the least affected by microbial attack [37–39]. An example of a partially degraded HPD diesel oil in soil is illustrated in Figure 6.38; 3 weeks after spiking, the intensity level of the *n*-alkanes is significantly reduced.

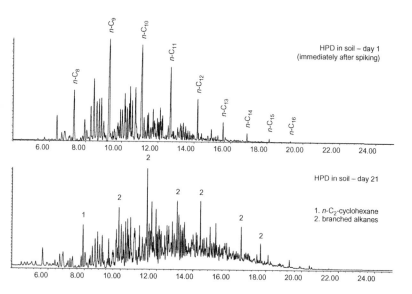

Figure 6.38 TICs of an HPD (diesel oil) in soil on day 1 and after 3 weeks (TD-GCMS).

A partially degraded straight-run HPD, showing a reduced intensity level of *n*-alkanes, may be difficult to distinguish from a partially dewaxed HPD. Indications for degradation rather than dewaxing may be found in the composition of the aromatics and perhaps branched alkanes.

6.3.4.6.3 Matrix/Pyrolysis Interference

Various burnt/pyrolyzed materials may release a series of *n*-alkanes. Examples of such materials are polyethylene (see Figure 5.1), fat (e.g., human/animal fat) [43], tar, and leather. The consecutive series of *n*-alkanes from these materials is usually accompanied by a series of *n*-alkenes and *n*-alkadienes, and sometimes by an additional series of aldehydes. Other compounds, such as aromatics, and alcohols in the case of burnt/pyrolyzed leather, may be released as well. Branched alkanes may be present, but for most burnt/pyrolyzed materials not in a pattern that is considered characteristic for crude oil. One exception is tar, which is a residue of the vacuum distillation of crude oil. In certain fire conditions, tar may release a combination of *n*-alkanes and branched alkanes in a pattern (including isoprenoids) that shows similarities with that of crude oil [44]. However, it can be distinguished from petroleum distillates by the presence of *n*-alkenes (these may be at a lower intensity level than the intensity of *n*-alkanes, depending on the fire conditions), and by the absence of cycloalkanes (no dominating *n*-alkylcyclohexanes at *m/z* 83).

Chromatograms of a burnt/pyrolyzed High Density Polyethylene are illustrated in Figure 6.39.

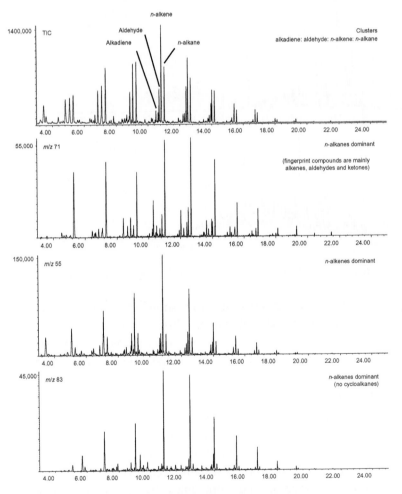

Figure 6.39 TIC and EICs of a burnt/pyrolyzed High Density Polyethylene (TD-GCMS).

6.3.4.7 Summary of Characteristics for the Identification of HPD

An HPD is characterized by the composition in Table 6.10, which should be demonstrated for a positive identification of an HPD in fire debris analysis results.

Table 6.10 Characteristics of a HPD			
Compound Family	Presence	Characteristics	Paragraph Reference
Alkanes	Present	A Gaussian-like[a] or consecutive distribution of normal-, branched-, and cycloalkanes predominantly in the range of C_9-C_{20+}, and spanning at least five[b] consecutive n-alkanes. n-Alkanes dominant, branched alkanes, and cycloalkanes (including isoprenoïds) in a characteristic crude oil fingerprint pattern at m/z 71, and cycloalkane(s) dominant at m/z 83.	6.3.4.2
Aromatics	Present in straight-run HPD, absent or present in insignificant amounts in de-aromatized HPD	Alkylbenzenes, indane and methylindanes, naphthalene and methylnaphtalenes are present in the corresponding carbon range	6.3.4.2
Oxygenates	Absent in straight-run HPD		

[a]*Exceptions can be diesel oil and heating oils, which are often blends of different refinery fractions (from primary and secondary distillation). As a result, the consecutive series of n-alkanes is dominantly present but does not represent a Gaussian-like distribution, as can be seen in Figure 6.30.*
[b]*It may be less than 5 in case of narrow-range products starting above n-C_{11}.*

HPD products designed for a specific application (i.e., fuel for diesel engines) can contain a blend fraction of biodiesel that consists of particular oxygenates: Fatty acids esters (mainly $C_{16}-C_{18}$ FAMEs); see paragraphs 6.3.4.1 and 6.3.4.2. These FAMEs support the identification of an HPD diesel fuel, when identified in fire debris analysis results in combination with the above listed characteristics of a straight-run HPD.

If one or more of the HPD characteristics are not met, further explanations for the presence of the identified components in the fire debris analysis results should be considered. For example:

- The absence (or reduced presence) of n-alkanes may indicate microbial degradation; see paragraph 6.3.4.6.
- The absence of n-alkanes (or reduced presence) and aromatics may indicate a Naphthenic-Paraffinic Product; see paragraph 6.6.

- The absence of *n*-alkanes, cycloalkanes, and aromatics may indicate an Isoparaffinic Product; see paragraph 6.4.
- The absence of a characteristic crude oil (fingerprint) pattern (including cycloalkanes and isoprenoïds) and aromatics may indicate a Normal Alkane-Isoparaffinic Product of class "Other-Miscellaneous"; see paragraph 6.9.
- The abundant presence of other types of components may indicate a technical solvent of class "Oxygenated Solvents" or "Other-Miscellaneous"; see paragraphs 6.8 and 6.9.

6.3.5 "Light to Medium" and "Medium to Heavy" Petroleum Distillates

The boiling range of some petroleum distillates does not fit neatly into one of the three subclasses defined by ASTM E1618. These products should be classified as "light to medium", or "medium to heavy" petroleum distillates. An example of a medium to heavy product, sold as "petroleum" is illustrated in Figure 6.40.

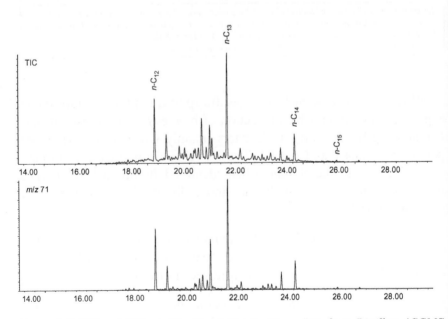

Figure 6.40 TIC and EIC m/z *71 of a Medium to Heavy Petroleum Distillate (GCMS of pentane dilutions).*

6.3.6 Composition of Petroleum Distillates Compared Isoparaffinic Products

Isoparaffinic Products consist almost exclusively of branched alkanes. They differ from petroleum distillates in composition, which is evident in the absence (or insignificant level) of *n*-alkanes, cycloalkanes, and aromatics. Furthermore, compared to petroleum distillates, the branched alkane pattern is not characteristic for crude oil. Three different examples of Isoparaffinic Products (sold as "petroleum", "thinner", and "lamp oil", respectively) compared to a conventional MPD are illustrated in Figure 6.41a and b.

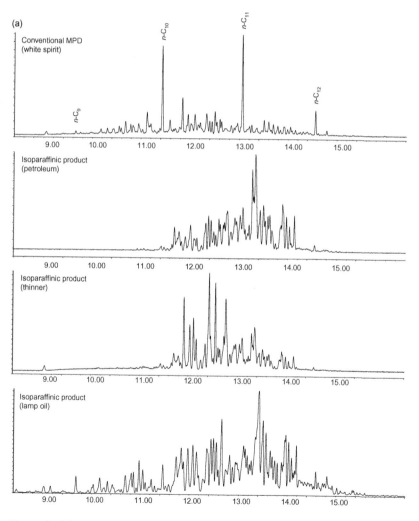

Figure 6.41 (a) TIC of a conventional MPD and three Isoparaffinic Products (TD-GCMS). (b) EIC m/z 71 of a conventional MPD and three Isoparaffinic Products (TD-GCMS).

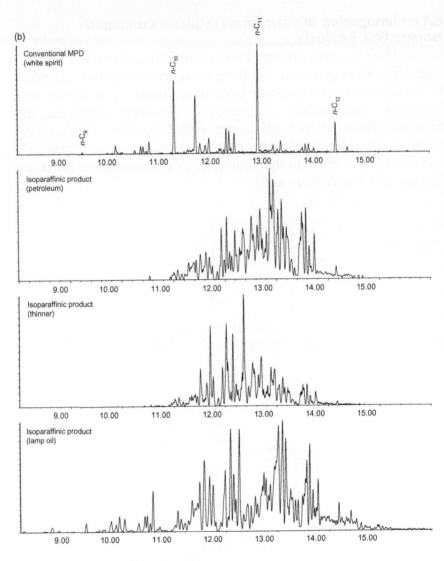

Figure 6.41 (Continued)

6.3.7 Composition of Petroleum Distillates Compared to Normal Alkane-Isoparaffinic Products

Normal Alkane-Isoparaffinic Products consist of normal and branched alkanes. Cycloalkanes and aromatics are absent. They differ from petroleum distillates in the composition of the branched alkanes (pattern is not characteristic for crude oil), and in the absence of isoprenoïds (present in crude oil). These differences indicate that the Normal Alkane-Isoparaffinic products are produced synthetically.

An example of a Normal Alkane-Isoparaffinic Product (sold as "lamp oil") compared to a conventional HPD (sold as "petroleum") is illustrated in Figure 6.42a−c. The composition of the branched alkanes in this lamp oil is similar to that of GTL diesels, indicating that this lamp oil may have been obtained through a Fischer-Tropsch process (see paragraph 3.3.1).

Examples of Normal Alkane-Isoparaffinic Products with compositions other than the lamp oil illustrated here, are discussed and illustrated in paragraphs 6.7.2 and 6.9.

Ignitable liquid compositions that resemble a mixture of classes, fall into class Other-Miscellaneous.

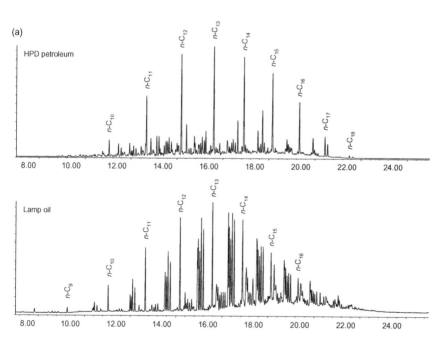

Figure 6.42 (a) TIC of conventional HPD and Normal Alkane-Isoparaffinic Product (TD-GCMS). (b) EIC m/z 71 of conventional HPD and Normal Alkane-Isoparaffinic Product (TD-GCMS). (c) EIC m/z 83 of conventional HPD and Normal Alkane-Isoparaffinic Product (TD-GCMS).

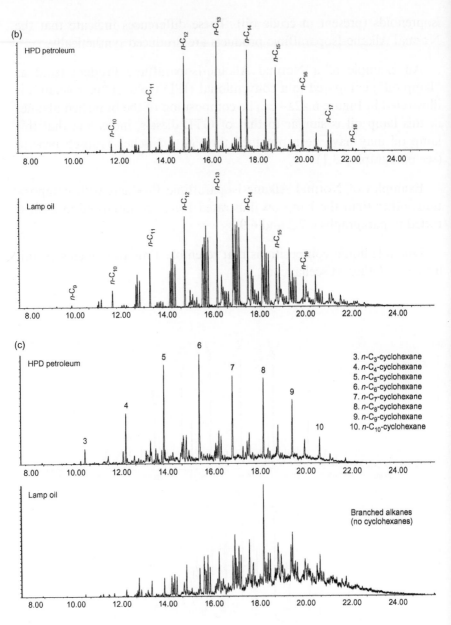

Figure 6.42 (Continued)

6.3.8 Petroleum Distillates in Technical Solvents

Petroleum distillates can be part of the composition of a commercially available ignitable liquid, often produced and sold for specific applications. Four examples of such commercial products are illustrated in

Figure 6.43. One is sold as "brush cleaner" and three are sold as "sticker remover". The compositions of the first two technical solvents fall into the class "Other-Miscellaneous", the last two examples should be considered an Oxygenated Solvent due to the major presence of IPA and butyl acetate, respectively.

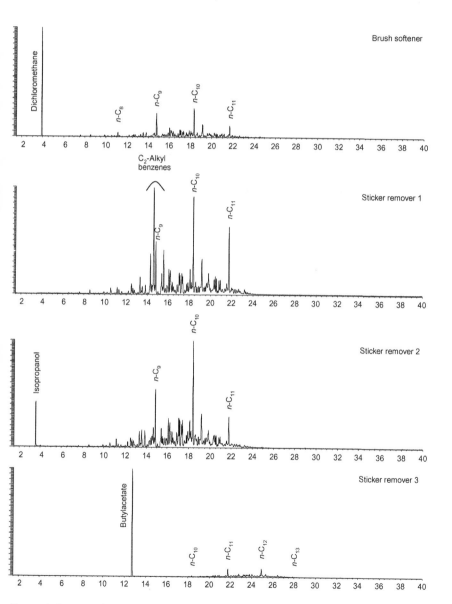

Figure 6.43 TICs of ignitable liquid products containing a petroleum distillate as ingredient (HS-GCMS 2).

Note. The first example in Figure 6.43 illustrates the composition of an old brush softener, which contains dichloromethane. Nowadays, the marketing and use of dichloromethane-based products is restricted [45]. Today's brush softeners and paint removers consist mainly of oxygenated compounds, an example is illustrated in paragraph 6.8 (Figure 6.56).

Petroleum Distillates can also be used as a technical solvent in certain commercial products. Examples of such products are glue, furniture polish, shoe polish, copper polish, and roof primers. Examples of a technical solvent in different commercially available products are illustrated in Figure 6.44. Whether or not the petroleum distillate in such commercial products is ignitable at ambient temperatures, depends on the concentration of the distillate.

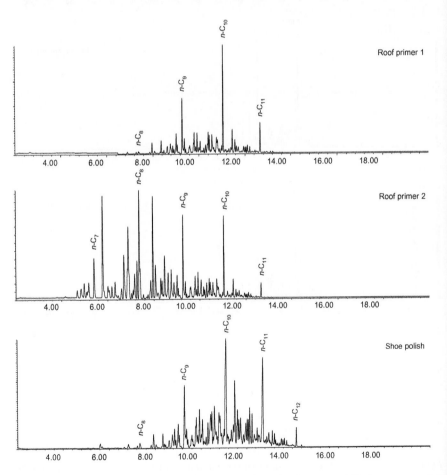

Figure 6.44 TICs of petroleum distillates as technical solvents in different commercial products (TD-GCMS).

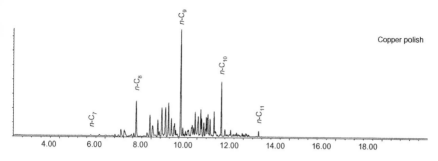

Copper polish

Figure 6.44 (Continued)

6.4 ISOPARAFFINIC PRODUCTS

6.4.1 Introduction

Isoparaffinic products consist almost exclusively of branched alkanes. The composition (pattern) is different from, or does not show enough characteristics of crude oil, and is governed by the production process(es) employed. The boiling range may vary, and is determined by the specifications of the end product. *n*-Alkanes, cycloalkanes, and aromatics are absent, or present in insignificant amounts.

Isoparaffinic products are produced synthetically[16]. Different processes are known, one is the Fisher-Tropsch process discussed in paragraph 3.3.1, and the other is an alkylation process [46].

TIC and EIC chromatograms of a Medium Isoparaffinic Product (sold as "lamp oil") with a composition that consists almost exclusively of C_9-C_{13} branched alkanes, are illustrated in Figure 6.45.

---

[16] To the author's present understanding.

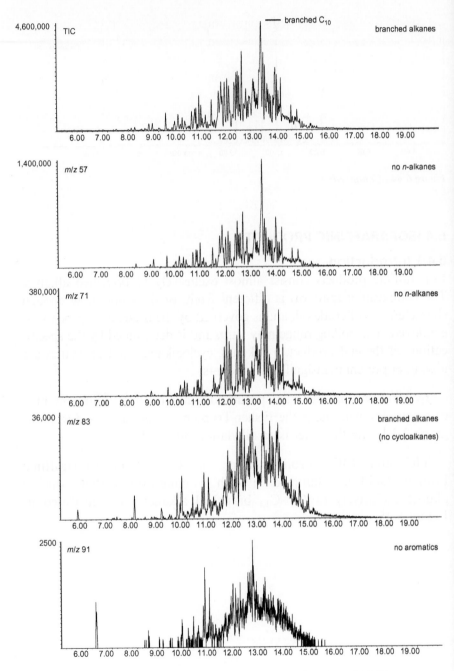

Figure 6.45 TIC and EICs of a Medium Isoparaffinic Product (TD-GCMS).

Another example of an Isoparaffinic Product is Alkylate gasoline. This is a motor gasoline, which is often referred to as "cleaner burning gasoline" or "green gasoline" due to its low aromatic content. The composition of alkylate gasoline compared to conventional gasoline is discussed and illustrated in paragraph 6.2.6. Two more examples of alkylate gasolines (with negligible aromatic content) are illustrated in Figure 6.46.

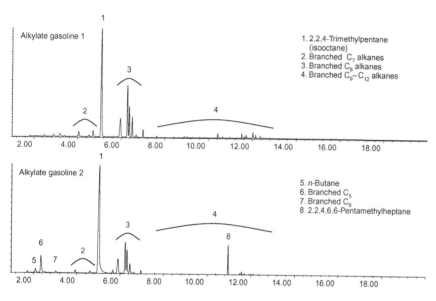

Figure 6.46 TICs of Isoparaffinic Products (both sold as "alkylate gasoline"; TD-GCMS).

6.4.2 Composition of Isoparaffinic Products Compared to (De-Aromatized) Petroleum Distillates

Isoparaffinic products differ from petroleum distillates in composition, which is evident in the absence (or insignificant level) of n-alkanes, cycloalkanes (and aromatics). Compared to petroleum distillates, the branched alkane pattern is not characteristic for crude oil. Three different examples of Isoparaffinic Products (sold as "petroleum", "thinner", and "lamp oil") compared to a conventional MPD are illustrated in paragraph 6.3.6 (Figure 6.41).

6.4.3 Composition of Normal Alkane-Isoparaffinic Products

Isoparaffinic products can be part of the composition of a commercially available ignitable liquid product, often produced and sold for specific applications.

On the Dutch market, lamp oils are a typical example of ignitable liquids, which consist of a blend of Normal Alkanes with an Isoparaffinic Product. They fall into the class "Other-Miscellaneous". One example of such a lamp oil is illustrated in Figure 6.47. More examples are illustrated in paragraph 6.9, showing the variety in blend compositions of these products.

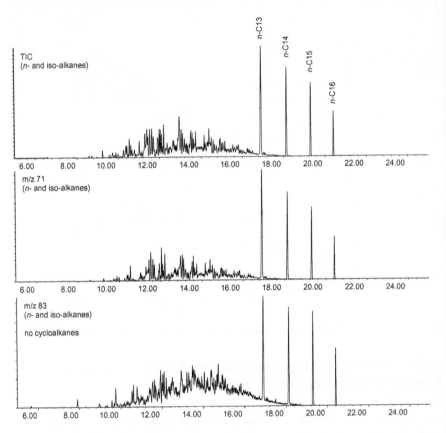

Figure 6.47 TIC and EIC m/z 71 *and* m/z 83 *of a Normal Alkane-Isoparaffinic Product, sold as "lamp oil" (TD-GCMS).*

The branched alkane pattern of these products is atypical for crude oil. Cycloalkanes are absent. Aromatics are absent.

6.4.4 Summary of Characteristics for the Identification of Isoparaffinic Products

An Isoparaffinic Product is characterized by the composition in Table 6.11, which should be demonstrated for a positive identification of an Isoparaffinic Product in fire debris analysis results.

Table 6.11 Characteristics of an Isoparaffinic Product

Compound Family	Presence	Characteristics	Paragraph Reference
Alkanes	Present	A range of almost exclusively branched alkanes, in a pattern that can be expected for an Isoparaffinic Product and which is different from and not characteristic for crude oil. n-Alkanes and cycloalkanes are absent, or present in insignificant amounts. The boiling range may vary.	6.4.1; 6.3.6
Aromatics	Absent, or present in insignificant amounts		
Oxygenates	Absent		

If the characteristics of an Isoparaffinic Product are not met, further explanations for the presence of the identified components in the fire debris analysis results should be considered. For example:

- The presence of cycloalkanes may indicate a Naphthenic-Paraffinic Product; see paragraph 6.6.
- The presence of n-alkanes may indicate a Normal Alkane-Isoparaffinic Product of class "Other-Miscellaneous"; see paragraph 6.9.
- The abundant presence of other types of components, may indicate a technical solvent of class "Oxygenated Solvents" or "Other-Miscellaneous"; see paragraphs 6.8 and 6.9.

6.5 AROMATIC PRODUCTS

6.5.1 Introduction
Aromatic Products consist almost exclusively of aromatic and/or condensed ring aromatic compounds. Alkanes are absent, or present in insignificant amounts. The composition and boiling range may vary, and are determined by the specifications of the end product.

An example of a commercially available product, containing an Aromatic Product as a technical solvent (which is ignitable) is discussed in paragraph 6.2.5, and illustrated in Figure 6.16. This example represents the technical solvent in a product sold as "roof primer". TIC chromatograms of other Aromatic Product examples are illustrated in Figure 6.48.

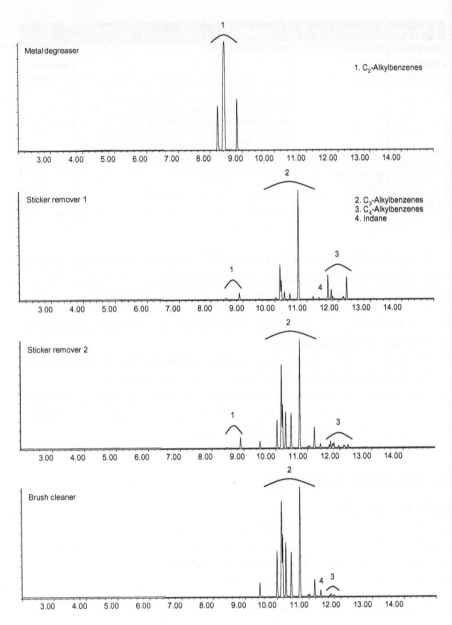

Figure 6.48 TICs of different Aromatic Products (TD-GCMS).

6.5.2 Composition of Aromatic Product Compared to Gasoline

The composition of an Aromatic Product can resemble the composition of a heavily weathered gasoline. As a result, both may be indistinguishable. An example is given in paragraph 6.2.5 (Figure 6.17). It represents the technical solvent in a product sold as "roof primer".

6.5.3 Aromatic Products in Technical Solvents

Aromatic Products can be applied as technical solvents in certain commercial/industrial products. In addition to the example given in the preceding paragraph, Figure 6.49 shows five more examples, sold as "racing fuel", "brush cleaning thinner", "sticker remover", "stain remover", and "roof and gutter sealant", respectively. Whether or not the technical solvent in such products is ignitable at ambient temperatures, depends, amongst others factors, upon the concentration of the solvent. The composition of the racing fuel, the brush cleaning thinner, the sticker remover, and the technical solvent in the roof and gutter sealant falls into the class "Other-Miscellaneous". The technical solvent in the stain remover can be classified as "Aromatic Product".

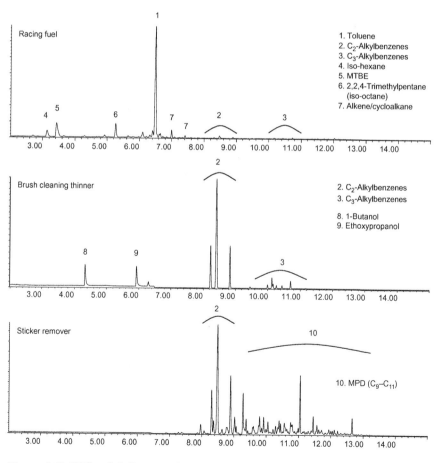

Figure 6.49 TICs of different technical solvents containing an Aromatic Product as ingredient (TD-GCMS).

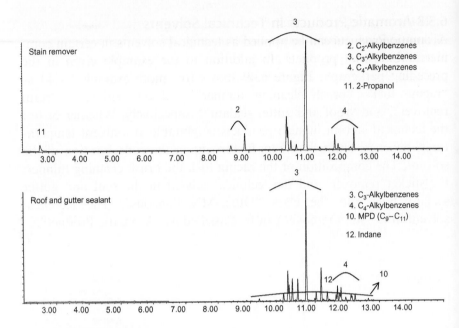

Figure 6.49 (Continued)

6.5.4 Matrix Interference

Aromatic compounds are released from various combusted and/or pyrolyzed materials, as discussed in Chapter 5. Caution is needed to avoid misinterpreting them and identifying them as false positives in fire debris samples.

6.5.5 Summary of Characteristics for the Identification of Aromatic Products

An Aromatic Product is characterized by the composition in Table 6.12, which should be demonstrated for a positive identification of an Aromatic Product in fire debris analysis results.

Table 6.12 Characteristics of an Aromatic Product			
Compound Family	Presence	Characteristics	Paragraph Reference
Alkanes	Absent, or present in insignificant amounts		
Aromatics	Present	Composition and boiling range may vary	6.5.1; 6.5.2
Oxygenates	Absent, or present in insignificant amounts		

If the aromatic components are identified together with other type of components, further explanations for the presence of the identified aromatics in the fire debris analysis results should be considered. For example:

- The presence of C_4-C_9 (and perhaps C_{12}) alkanes (in a pattern that can be expected for gasoline) and/or oxygenates (added to gasoline) may indicate Gasoline; see paragraph 6.2.
- The abundant presence of other types of components may indicate a technical solvent of the class "Oxygenated Solvents" or "Other-Miscellaneous"; see paragraphs 6.8 and 6.9.
- The presence of typical pyrolysis indicators (such as benzene, styrene, alkenes) may indicate pyrolysis products.

6.6 NAPHTHENIC-PARAFFINIC PRODUCTS

6.6.1 Introduction

Naphthenic-Paraffinic Products consist mainly of branched and cycloalkanes. n-Alkanes are absent, or present at lowered levels compared to petroleum distillates. Aromatics are absent, or present in insignificant amounts. The composition and boiling range may vary, and are determined by the specifications of the end product.

An example of a Naphthenic-Paraffinic Product is discussed in paragraph 6.3.3.4 and illustrated in Figure 6.28. This example is sold as "Odourless white spirit". Another example, sold as "Barbeque lighter fluid", is illustrated in Figure 6.50. Both these products consist mainly of branched alkanes and cycloalkanes, with n-alkanes present at lowered levels compared to petroleum distillates, and aromatics are absent.

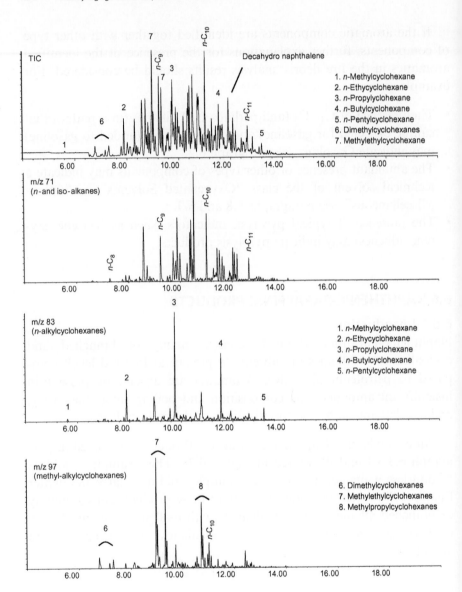

Figure 6.50 TIC and EICs of a Naphthenic-Paraffinic Product, sold as "barbeque lighter fluid" (TD-GCMS).

6.6.2 Naphthenic-Paraffinic Products in Technical Solvents

Naphthenic-Paraffinic Products can be blended with other types of components and/or products from other classes to form a technical solvent for certain commercial/industrial products. Four examples of such technical solvents in commercially available products sold as "correction fluid", "stain remover" and "contact glue" are illustrated in Figure 6.51. The ignitability at ambient temperatures of a technical solvent in commercially/industrially available products depends, amongst other factors, upon the concentration of the solvent. The technical solvent in all four examples is ignitable. The compositions of these technical solvents fall into the class "Other-Miscellaneous".

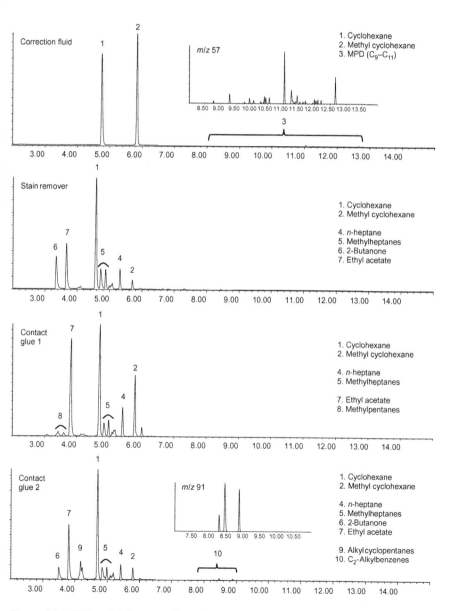

Figure 6.51 TICs of different technical solvents in commercial products, containing a Naphthenic-Paraffinic Product as ingredient (TD-GCMS).

6.6.3 Summary of Characteristics for the Identification of Naphthenic-Paraffinic Products

A Naphthenic-Paraffinic Product is characterized by the composition in Table 6.13, which should be demonstrated for a positive identification of a Naphthenic-Paraffinic Product in fire debris analysis results.

Table 6.13 Characteristics of a Naphthenic-Paraffinic Product			
Compound Family	Presence	Characteristics	Paragraph Reference
Alkanes	Present	Almost exclusively branched alkanes and cycloalkanes. n-Alkanes are absent, or present at lowered levels compared to petroleum distillates. The composition/pattern and boiling range may vary.	6.6.1; 6.6.2
Aromatics	Absent, or present in insignificant amounts		
Oxygenates	Absent		

If the characteristics for a Naphthenic-Paraffinic Product are not met, further explanations for the presence of the identified components in the fire debris analysis results should be considered. For example:

- The abundant presence of n-alkanes may indicate a Petroleum Distillate; see paragraph 6.3.
- The absence of cycloalkanes may indicate an Isoparaffinic Product; see paragraph 6.4.
- The abundant presence of other types of components may indicate a technical solvent of the class "Oxygenated Solvents" or "Other-Miscellaneous"; see paragraphs 6.8 and 6.9.

6.7 NORMAL ALKANE PRODUCTS

6.7.1 Introduction

Normal Alkane Products consist almost exclusively of n-alkanes. Branched alkanes and cycloalkanes are absent, or present at insignificant levels. Aromatics are absent. The boiling range may vary, and is determined by the specifications of the end product.

TIC and EIC chromatograms of different Normal Alkane Products are illustrated in Figure 6.52. These products are sold as "lamp oil", "torch oil", and "barbecue fluid".

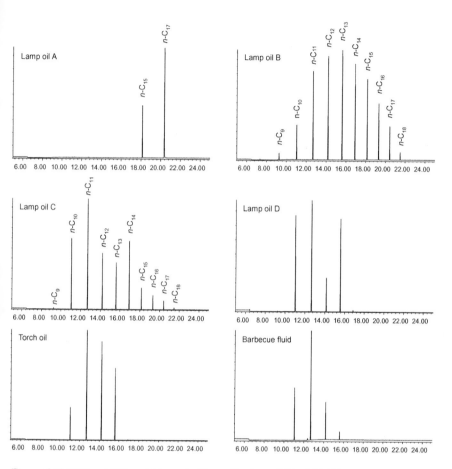

Figure 6.52 TICs of different Normal Alkane Products (TD-GCMS).

6.7.2 Composition of Normal Alkane-Isoparaffinic Products

Normal Alkane Products can be part of the composition of an ignitable liquid product, such as a Normal Alkane-Isoparaffinic Product, produced and sold for specific applications. A typical example of such a product on the Dutch market is lamp oil, as already mentioned in paragraph 6.4.3. This example is reproduced in Figure 6.53. More examples are discussed in paragraph 6.9, and illustrated in Figure 6.63.

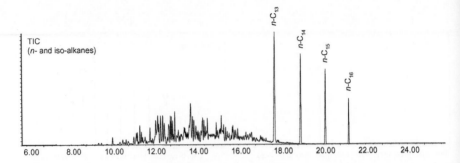

Figure 6.53 TIC of a Normal Alkane-Isoparaffinic Product, sold as "lamp oil" (TD-GCMS).

6.7.3 Normal Alkane Products in Technical Solvents

Normal Alkane Products can also be used as technical solvents in certain commercially/industrially available products. An example of such a product is fire starters, based on urea formaldehyde. Another example is carbonless forms [27], in which a Normal Alkane Product can be applied as technical solvent. The amount of Normal Alkane Product in the first example (fire starters) is ignitable, in the second example (carbonless forms) it is not.

In carbonless forms, the Normal Alkane Product is often identified together with substituted biphenyls [27]. This combination can be used as an indicator in the interpretation and conclusion step of fire debris analysis results.

6.7.4 Matrix Interference

Certain substrate materials can release a series of n-alkanes, in a composition that may resemble that of certain Normal Alkane Products. Caution is necessary to avoid misinterpreting and reporting these as such without further comment.

An example of such a substrate is unburned polyethylene (PE) material. During the thermal processing (extrusion, etc.) of these materials, they can release a series of n-alkanes as degradation products [47] under certain conditions. Two examples of the volatiles recovered from the heated (70 °C) headspace of unburned PE bags, compared to the technical solvent in a white barbecue lighter block are shown in Figure 6.54. The technical solvent in the barbecue lighter block can be classified as Normal Alkane Product, if the level of branched alkanes is considered "insignificant". Otherwise, class "Other-Miscellaneous" should be considered instead.

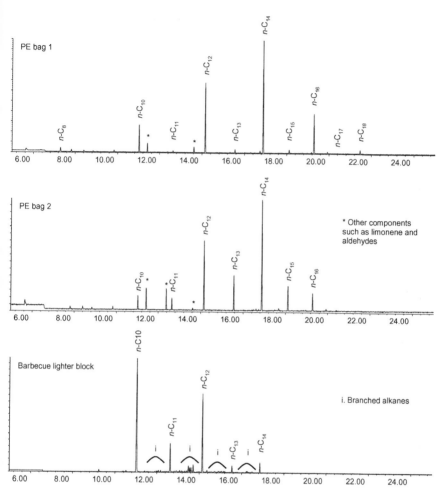

Figure 6.54 TICs of two unburned PE bags compared to a Normal Alkane-Isoparaffinic Product (sold as "white barbecue lighter block"; TD-GCMS).

6.7.5 Summary of Characteristics for the Identification of Normal Alkane Products

A Normal Alkane Product is characterized by the composition in Table 6.14, which should be demonstrated for a positive identification of a Normal Alkane Product in fire debris analysis results.

Table 6.14 Characteristics of a Normal Alkane Product

Compound Family	Presence	Characteristics	Paragraph Reference
Alkanes	Present	A range of (almost) exclusively *n*-alkanes. Branched alkanes and cycloalkanes are absent, or present in insignificant amounts. The boiling range may vary.	6.7.1
Aromatics	Absent		
Oxygenates	Absent		

If the characteristics for a Normal Alkane Product are not met, further explanations for the presence of the identified components in the fire debris analysis results should be considered. For example:

• The presence of branched alkanes may indicate a Normal Alkane-Isoparaffinic Product of class "Other-Miscellaneous", see paragraph 6.9.

6.8 OXYGENATED SOLVENTS

6.8.1 Introduction

Oxygenated solvents contain major oxygenated components, such as alcohols, esters, and/or ketones. Other types of components (e.g., alkanes, aromatics) or distillate fractions can be present, but not necessarily as major components.

TIC chromatograms of different Oxygenated Solvents are illustrated in Figures 6.55–6.57.

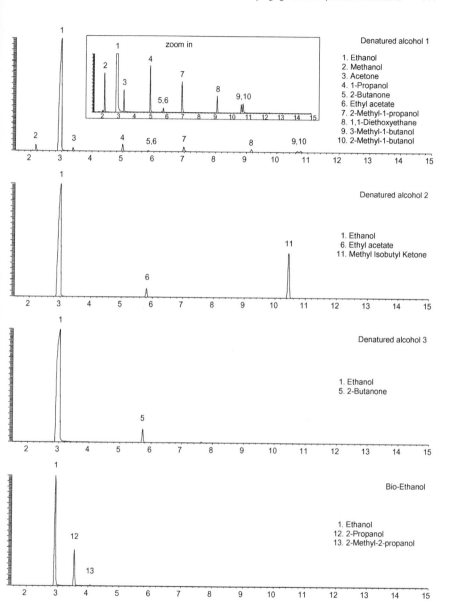

Figure 6.55 TICs of different Oxygenated Solvents (sold as "Denatured Alcohol" and "Bio-ethanol"; HS-GCMS 2).

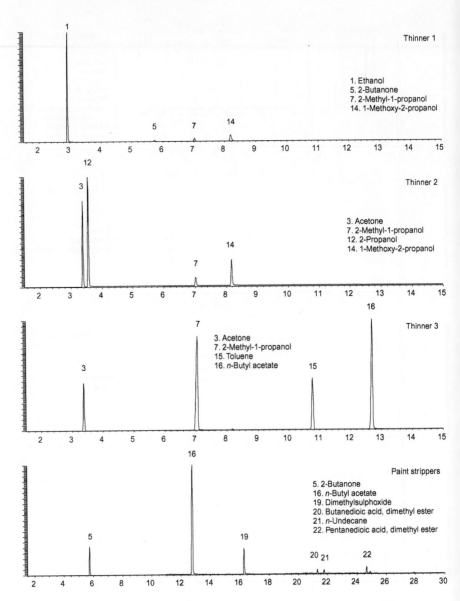

Figure 6.56 TICs of different Oxygenated Solvents (sold as "Thinner" and "Paint strippers"; HS-GCMS 2).

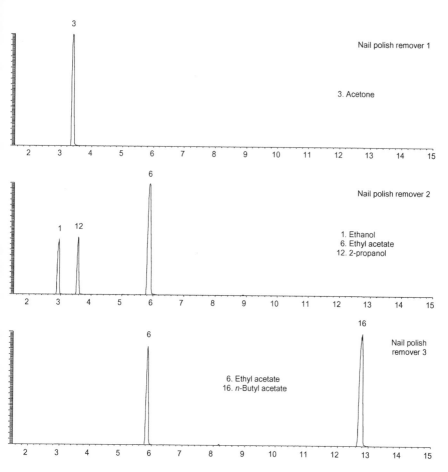

Figure 6.57 TICs of different Oxygenated Solvents (all three sold as "Nail polish remover"; HS-GCMS 2).

6.8.2 Oxygenated Compounds/Solvents in Technical Solvents

Oxygenated Solvents can also be used as technical solvents in certain commercially/industrially available products. Examples of such products are fire gels and pastes, based on modified cellulose or polyacrylate. An oxygenated compound or solvent can be used as the technical solvent in glues, detergents, perfume and cosmetic products, etc. The ignitability at ambient temperatures of a technical solvent in commercially/industrially available products depends, amongst other factors, upon the concentration of the solvent.

Three examples of oxygenated solvents, used in different commercial products (sold as "fire paste", "fire gel", and "universal glue", respectively), are illustrated in Figure 6.58. The oxygenated solvents in these three examples are present in ignitable amounts.

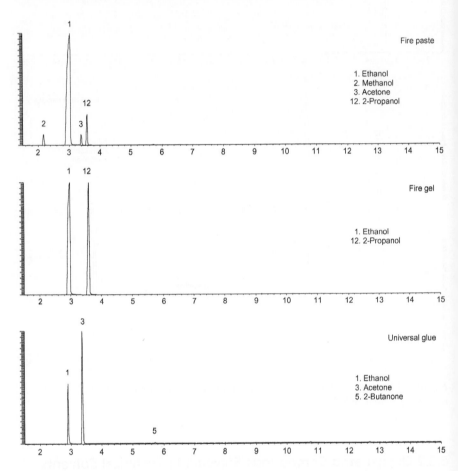

Figure 6.58 TICs of different Oxygenated Solvents as technical solvents in consumer products (sold as "fire paste", "fire gel", and "universal glue"; HS-GCMS 2).

Oxygenated compounds are also present in alcoholic drinks, such as beer, wine, and whisky, with ethanol being the main component. Other oxygenated compounds may be present as well. They are by-products of the fermentation process. An example of an alcoholic drink, red wine, is illustrated in Figure 6.59. The ignitability at ambient temperatures of alcoholic drinks depends on the percentage of ethanol amongst other factors. Whiskey is ignitable whereas wine is not.

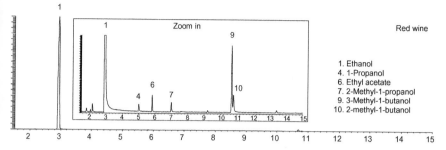

Figure 6.59 TIC of an alcoholic drink (sold as "red wine"; HS-GCMS 2).

6.8.3 Matrix Interference

6.8.3.1 Microbial Degradation

Oxygenated compounds can be subject to microbial degradation. An example of an oxygenated solvent, consisting of a combination of major oxygenated compounds and major aromatics, is illustrated in Figure 6.60. This product is sold as "thinner". One week after being spiked to soil, *n*-butyl acetate from the original thinner is no longer recovered.

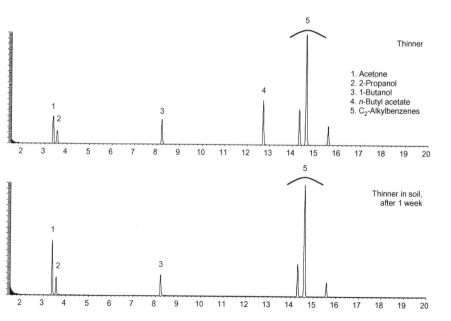

Figure 6.60 TICs of thinner and thinner recovered from soil after 1 week (HS-GCMS 2).

6.8.3.2 Matrix Interference

Oxygenated compounds can be released from various combusted and/ or pyrolyzed materials, as already discussed in Chapter 5. They can also be formed and released as a result of other processes that can take place after the fire has been extinguished. For example, as a result of fermentation processes occurring in wet plant material such as grass and hay. Caution is necessary to avoid misinterpreting and classifying them as false positives in fire debris samples.

A TIC example of hay, 1 week after wetting, is illustrated in Figure 6.61. Caution is necessary to avoid interpreting the volatiles from wetted plant material as originating from a denatured alcohol product (see Figure 6.55, top), or an alcoholic drink (see Figure 6.59). As 1-butanol is abundantly present in samples of wetted plant material but absent in commonly encountered (denatured) alcohol products (in the Netherlands, Belgium, France, and Germany) it may be used as an indicator for the presence of wetted plant material.

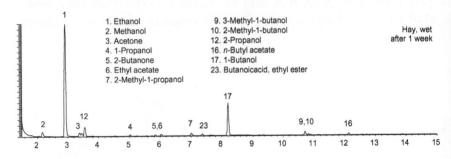

Figure 6.61 TIC of hay, 1 week after wetting (HS-GCMS 2).

6.8.4 Summary of Characteristics for the Identification of Oxygenated Solvents

An Oxygenated Solvent is characterized by the composition in Table 6.15.

Table 6.15 Characteristics of an Oxygenated Solvent			
Compound Family	Presence	Characteristics	Paragraph Reference
Alkanes	Can be present	Composition, boiling range, and concentration level may vary	
Aromatics	Can be present	Composition, boiling range, and concentration level may vary	
Oxygenates	Present	Major compound(s). Composition and boiling range may vary.	6.8.1; 6.8.2

Oxygenated Solvents may be present in fire debris when the characteristics listed above are met. However, the following should also be taken into consideration:

• Oxygenated compounds are present in many consumer and household products, such as detergents and cosmetics. They can also be released from various burnt, pyrolyzed, and/or fermented materials. To avoid false positive identifications, it is recommended to report on the presence of oxygenated compounds only when they are identified in significant amounts and/or identified in compositions which resemble those of known products.

6.9 OTHER-MISCELLANEOUS

6.9.1 Introduction

There are many ignitable liquids and commercially available products containing an ignitable liquid (technical solvent) as ingredient, the compositions of which do not neatly fall into one of the previously defined classes, or can fall into more than one of these. Some examples have already been discussed in previous paragraphs to illustrate the similarities and differences between them and the defined classes. To complete the picture these examples are also illustrated in Figure 6.62.

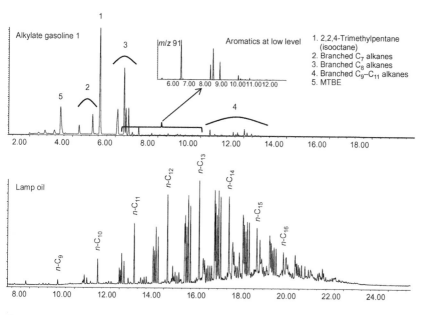

Figure 6.62 TICs of different technical solvents classified as Other-Miscellaneous (TD-GCMS).

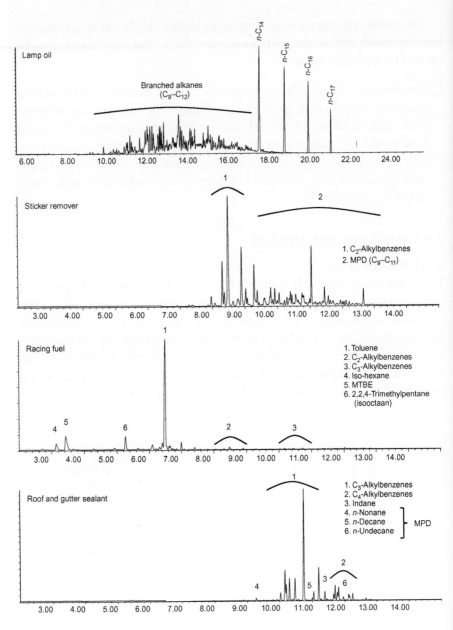

Figure 6.62 (Continued)

The second lamp oil example in Figure 6.62 clearly consists of a blend of a Normal Alkane-Isoparaffinic Product. These products are common on the Dutch market. ASTM E1618 has not defined a class for these products, according to this classification scheme they fall into class "Other-Miscellaneous". As already mentioned, they consist only of n-alkanes (a Normal Alkane Product) and branched alkanes (an Isoparaffinic Product). Cycloalkanes and aromatics are absent. The pattern of the branched alkanes is different from that of crude oil, indicating that this fraction is produced synthetically. In some products[17] this pattern is similar to that in GTL diesels (see example in paragraph 6.3.7), indicating that it may have been obtained through a Fisher-Tropsch process (see paragraph 3.3.1). Other known synthetic processes for Isoparaffinic Products are through an alkylation process [46].

The blend composition in these lamp oils varies. Examples with different blend compositions are illustrated in Figure 6.63. The first two examples contain only minor levels of an Isoparaffinic fraction. For these two products a classification as Normal Alkane Product can be considered instead.

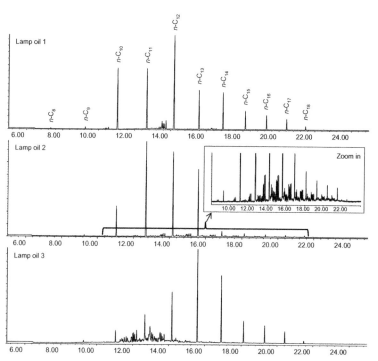

Figure 6.63 TICs of Normal Alkane-Isoparaffinic Products (all sold as "lamp oil"; TD-GCMS).

[17] This also applies to the first lamp oil example in Figure 6.62.

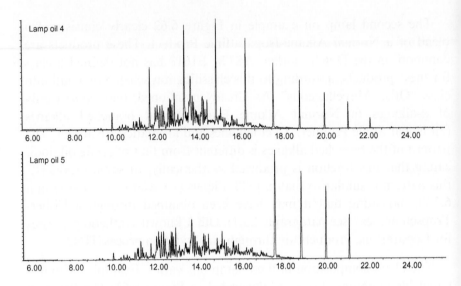

Figure 6.63 (Continued)

More examples of technical solvents that belong to the class "Other-Miscellaneous" are illustrated in Figure 6.64. These solvents may be available on the market as such or can be present in a commercial product such as correction fluid. The ignitability at ambient temperatures of a technical solvent in commercially/industrially available products depends upon the concentration of the solvent amongst other factors.

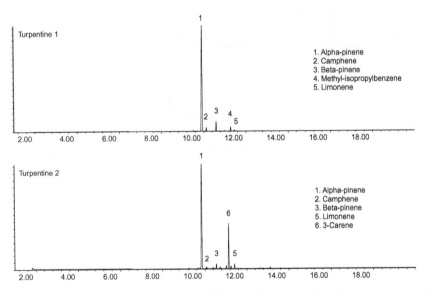

Figure 6.64 TICs of different technical solvents classified as Other-Miscellaneous (TD-GCMS).

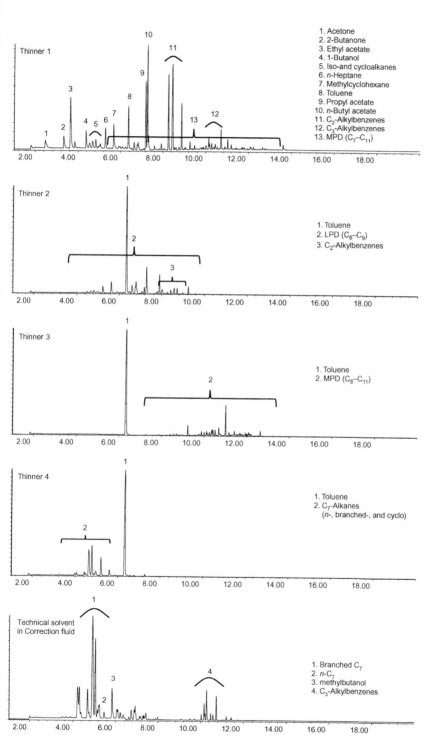

Figure 6.64 (Continued)

6.9.2 Matrix Interference

The enormous variation in the composition of ignitable liquids and technical solvents in the class "Other-Miscellaneous" combined with the wide variety of compounds that can be released from the substrate material(s) present in a fire debris sample (e.g., as a result of natural presence, combustion/pyrolysis, natural processes such as fermentation, etc.), can complicate the identification of these ignitable liquids or technical solvents. It is recommended that the presence of such products is reported only when they are identified in significant amounts, and preferably in compositions which resemble those of known products in order to avoid false positive identifications.

Some ignitable liquid products in the class "Other-Miscellaneous" have a natural origin, as for example, the ignitable liquid product sold as "turpentine" (see examples in Figure 6.64). It is obtained from the oil resin of certain plant materials and trees (mainly pines), and is composed of terpenes. Because of their natural origin, these terpenes are released from plant material or softwood, containing this resin, as well. Therefore, caution is necessary when terpenes are identified in a fire debris sample. When reported, they should be reported with a comment.

6.9.3 Summary of Characteristics for the Identification of an Ignitable Liquid from the Class "Other-Miscellaneous"

The class "Other-Miscellaneous" is meant for those ignitable liquid products and technical solvents, the composition of which either falls in none, or in more than one of the defined classes of ASTM E1618.

Some ignitable liquid products in the class "Other-Miscellaneous" are composed of mixtures of products from other ASTM E1618 classes. Examples are some sticker removers and lamp oils (see Figure 6.62). When identifying this in fire debris analysis results, one should consider reporting the identified products separately, with a notation that such a composition is applied as technical solvent for a specific application (in the examples, as sticker remover and lamp oil).

It is recommended that the (possible) presence of a product from the class "Other-Miscellaneous" is reported only when the compounds are identified in significant amounts, and/or in compositions which resemble those of known products in order to avoid false positive identifications.

Summary of GCMS Methods and Conditions

Neat liquid injection GCMS method (GCMS, direct injection)	
Injection volume	0.2 μL
Split ratio	1:500
Inlet temperature	275 °C
GC-column	Ultra 1 ms (25 m × 200 μm × 0.33 μm)
GC oven temperature program	35 °C/3 min−10 °C/min−250 °C/6 min
MS source temperature	230 °C

Solvent liquid injection GCMS method 1, solvent dilution (GCMS of pentane dilution)	
Injection volume	1 μL
Split ratio	1:50
Inlet temperature	275 °C
GC-column	Ultra 1 ms (25 m × 200 μm × 0.33 μm)
GC oven temperature program	35 °C/2 min−5 °C/min−200 °C/0 min, 15 °C/min−275 °C/0 min
MS source temperature	230 °C

Solvent liquid injection GCMS method 2, solvent extract of bricks (GCMS of isooctane extract)	
Injection volume	0.5 μL
Split ratio	1:20
Inlet temperature	275 °C
GC-column	Zebron ZB1-HT (30 m × 250 μm × 0.1 μm)
GC oven temperature program	40 °C/5 min−15 °C/min−320 °C/20 min
MS source temperature	180 °C

Static headspace GCMS method 1 (HS GCMS 1)

Injection volume	0.5 mL HS (70 °C)
Split ratio	1:10
Inlet temperature	275 °C
GC-column	Ultra 1 ms (25 m × 200 μm × 0.33 μm)
GC oven temperature program	35 °C/3 min−10 °C/min−250 °C/6 min
MS source temperature	230 °C

Static headspace GCMS method 2 (HS GCMS 2)

Injection volume	0.5 mL HS (70 °C)
Split ratio	1:10
Inlet temperature	200 °C
GC-column	DB624 (30 m × 250 μm × 1.4 μm)
GC oven temperature program	40 °C/2 min−5 °C/min−240 °C/6 min
MS source temperature	230 °C

Preconcentrated headspace (Tenax[R]) Thermal Desorption GCMS method (TD-GCMS)

Injection volume	5−100 mL HS (70 °C) on Tenax
Adsorbent	Tenax® TA
Front inlet temperature	250 °C
Back inlet temperature	175 °C
Split ratio	1:13.5 or 1:546
GC-column	Ultra 1 ms (25 m × 200 μm × 0.33 μm)
GC oven temperature program	35 °C/3 min−10 °C/min−250 °C/6 min
MS source temperature	230 °C

Passive headspace (SPME) GCMS method (SPME-GCMS)

Sampling time	x s−y min HS (70 °C) on SPME fiber
SPME fiber	100 μm PDMS, 75 μm CAR-PDMS
Split ratio	1:200
Inlet temperature	275 °C
GC-column	Ultra 1 ms (25 m × 200 μm × 0.33 μm)
GC oven temperature program	35 °C/2 min−10 °C/min−250 °C/6 min
MS source temperature	230 °C

REFERENCES

[1] ASTM E1618-14, Standard Test Method for Ignitable Liquid Residues in Extracts from Fire Debris Samples by Gas Chromatography-Mass Spectrometry, ASTM International, West Conshohocken, PA, 2014.

[2] R. Newman, M. Gilbert, K. Lothridge, GC-MS Guide to Ignitable Liquids, first ed., CRC Press LLC, Boca Raton, FL, 1998.

[3] Online Ignitable Liquids Reference Collection Database, National Center for Forensic Science, University of Central Florida. Available from: <http://ilrc.ucf.edu/>.

[4] NFPA® 921, Guide for Fire and Explosion Investigations, National Fire and Protection Association (NFPA), 2014.

[5] Globally Harmonized System of Classification and Labelling of Chemicals (GHS), fifth revised ed., United Nations, New York and Geneva, 2013.

[6] <http://en.wikipedia.org/wiki/Petroleum_product>.

[7] Directive 2009/28/EC of the European Parliament and of the Council on the promotion of the use of energy from renewable sources and amending and subsequently repealing Directives 2001/77/EC and 2003/30/EC.

[8] European Standard EN 590: 2010, Automotive Fuels—Diesel—Requirements and Test Methods.

[9] European Standard EN 228: 2012, Automotive Fuels—Unleaded Petrol—Requirements and Test Methods.

[10] <http://www.afdc.energy.gov/fuels/emerging_xtl_fuels.html>.

[11] <http://www.shell.com/global/products-services/solutions-for-businesses/chemicals/products/solvents/gas-to-liquids-solvents.html>.

[12] <http://www.shell.com/global/future-energy/natural-gas/gtl/products.html>.

[13] <http://biofuel.org.uk/>.

[14] Q. Ren, W. Bertsch, A comprehensive sample preparation scheme for accelerants in suspect arson cases, J. Forensic Sci. 44 (3) (1999) 504−515.

[15] W. Bertsch, Q. Ren, Contemporary sample preparation methods for the detection of ignitable liquids in suspect arson cases, Forensic Sci. Rev. 11 (2) (1999) 141−156.

[16] ASTM. E1318-10, Standard Practice for Separation of Ignitable Liquid Residues from Fire Debris Samples by Solvent Extraction, ASTM International, West Conshohocken, PA, 2010.

[17] ASTM. E1388-12, Standard Practice for Sampling of Headspace Vapors from Fire Debris Samples, ASTM International, West Conshohocken, PA, 2012.

[18] ASTM. E1412-12, Standard Practice for Separation of Ignitable Liquid Residues from Fire Debris Samples by Passive Headspace Concentration with Activated Charcoal, ASTM International, West Conshohocken, PA, 2012.

[19] ASTM. E1413-13, Standard Practice for Separation of Ignitable Liquid Residues from Fire Debris Samples by Dynamic Headspace Concentration, ASTM International, West Conshohocken, PA, 2013.

[20] ASTM. E2154-08, Standard Practice for Separation and Concentration of Ignitable Liquid Residues from Fire Debris Samples by Passive Headspace Concentration with Solid Phase Microextraction (SPME), ASTM International, West Conshohocken, PA, 2008.

[21] J.R. Almirall, K.G. Furton, Characterization of background and pyrolysis products that may interfere with the forensic analysis of fire debris, J. Anal. Appl. Pyrolysis 71 (2004) 51–67.

[22] Online Substrate Database, National Center for Forensic Science, University of Central Florida. Available from: <http://ilrc.ucf.edu/substrate/>.

[23] W. Bertsch, Q.-W. Zhang, Sample preparation for the chemical analysis of debris in suspect arson cases, Anal. Chim. Acta 236 (1990) 183–195.

[24] E. Stauffer, J.A. Dolan, R. Newman, Fire Debris Analysis, first ed., Academic Press, Elsevier, London, 2008 (Table 12-3)

[25] W. Bertsch, Volatiles from carpet: a source of frequent misinterpretation in analysis, J. Chromatogr. A 674 (1/2) (1994) 329–333.

[26] E. Stauffer, J.A. Dolan, R. Newman, Fire Debris Analysis, first ed., Academic Press, Elsevier, London, 2008 (Table 12-4)

[27] J.J. Lentini, J.A. Dolan, C. Cherry, The petroleum-laced background, J. Forensic Sci. 45 (5) (2000) 968–989.

[28] M. Fernandes, C. Lau, W. Wong, The effect of volatile residues in burnt household items on the detection of fire accelerants, Sci. Justice 42 (1) (2002) 7–15.

[29] E. Stauffer, Concept of pyrolysis for fire debris analysts, Sci. Justice 43 (1) (2003) 29–40.

[30] P.M.L. Sandercock, A survey of Canadian gasolines, J. Can. Soc. Forensic Sci. 40 (3) (2007) 105–130.

[31] P.M.L. Sandercock, Survey of Canadian gasoline (Winter 2010), J. Can. Soc. Forensic Sci. 45 (2) (2012) 64–78.

[32] L.J.C. Peschier, M.M.P. Grutters, J.N. Hendrikse, Using alkylate components for classifying gasoline in fire debris samples, submitted for publication.

[33] <http://ec.europa.eu/energy/res/legislation/doc/biofuels/en_final.pdf>.

[34] European Standard EN 228, Automotive Fuels—Unleaded Petrol—Requirements and Test Methods, 2012.

[35] <http://www.shell.com/global/products-services/solutions-for-businesses/globalsolutions/refinery-chemical-licensing/petrochemical-technology/pyrolsis-gasoline-processing.html>.

[36] DOW™ Product Safety Assessment, Pyrolysis Gasoline (Pygas), 2010.

[37] R. Marchal, S. Penet, F. Solano-Serena, J.P. Vandecasteele, Gasoline and diesel oil biodegradation, Oil Gas Sci. Technol. 58 (4) (2003) 441–448.

[38] D.A. Turner, J.V. Goodpaster, The effects of microbial degradation on ignitable liquids, Anal. Bioanal. Chem. 394 (2009) 363–371.

[39] D.A. Turner, J.V. Goodpaster, The effect of microbial degradation on the chromatographic profiles of tiki torch fuel, lamp oil, and turpentine, J. Forensic Sci. 56 (4) (2011) 984–987.

[40] <http://www.criterioncatalysts.com/content/dam/shell/static/criterion/downloads/pdf/fact-sheets/dewaxing-factsheethires.pdf>.

[41] Directive 2009/28/EC of the European Parliament and of the Council on the promotion of the use of energy from renewable sources and amending and subsequently repealing Directives 2001/77/EC and 2003/30/EC.

[42] K.E. Peters, C. Walters, J.M. Moldowan, second ed., The Biomarker Guide, Biomarkers and Isotopes in the Environmental and Human History, vol. 1, Cambridge University Press, Cambridge, 2005.

[43] J.D. DeHaan, D.J. Brien, R. Large, Volatile organic compounds from the combustion of human and animal tissue, Sci. Justice 44 (4) (2004) 223–236.

[44] J.J. Lentini, Differentiation of asphalt and smoke condensates from liquid petroleum distillates using GC/MS, J. Forensic Sci. 43 (1) (1998) 97–113.

[45] Decision 455/2009/EC of the European Parliament and of the Council amending Council Directive 76/769/EEC as regards restrictions on the marketing and use of dichloromethane.

[46] <http://www.shell.com/global/products-services/solutions-for-businesses/chemicals/products/solvents/hydrocarbon-solvents/isoparaffins/synthetic-isoparaffin.html>.

[47] T. Andersson, B. Ståhlbom, B. Wesslén, Degradation of polyethylene during extrusion. II. Degradation of low-density polyethylene, linear low-density polyethylene, and high-density polyethylene in film extrusion, J. Appl. Polym. Sci. 91 (2004) 1525–1537.

Printed and bound by CPI Group (UK) Ltd, Croydon, CR0 4YY

08/06/2025

01896868-0004